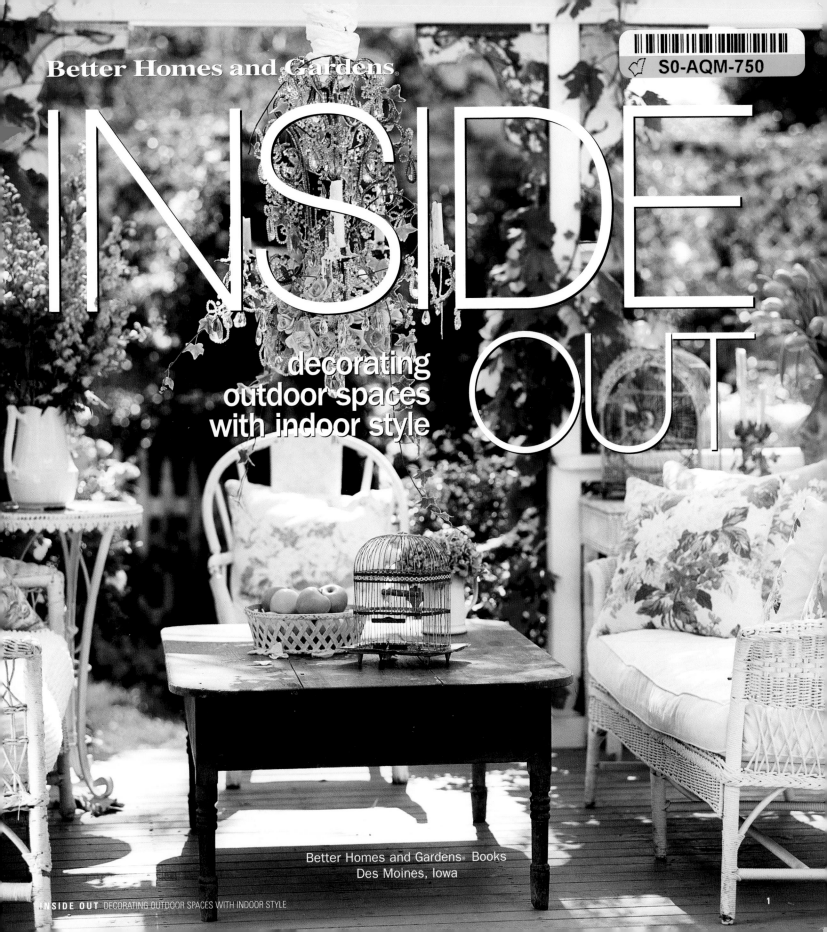

Better Homes and Gardens®

INSIDE
OUT

decorating
outdoor spaces
with indoor style

Better Homes and Gardens® Books
Des Moines, Iowa

Inside Out: Decorating Outdoor Spaces with Indoor Style
Editors: Vicki Ingham, Paula Marshall
Writer: Candace Ord Manroe
Art Director: Brad Ruppert
Contributing Editors: Diane Carroll, Helen Heitkamp, Linda Krinn,
    Karin Lidbeck, Sally Mauer
Copy Chief: Terri Fredrickson
Copy and Production Editor: Victoria Forlini
Editorial Operations Manager: Karen Schirm
Managers, Book Production: Pam Kvitne, Marjorie J. Schenkelberg, Rick von Holdt,
    Mark Weaver
Contributing Copy Editor: Stacey Schildroth
Contributing Proofreaders: Judy Friedman, Carol Boker, Sue Fetters
Contributing Photographers: Ross Chapple, Colleen Duffley, John Ellis, Randy Foulds,
    Jay Graham, Jamie Hadley, Robert Mauer, Tom McWilliams
Indexer: Kathleen Poole
Editorial and Design Assistants: Kaye Chabot, Karen McFadden, Mary Lee Gavin

Meredith® Books
Editor in Chief: Linda Raglan Cunningham
Design Director: Matt Strelecki
Executive Editor, Home Decorating and Design: Denise L. Caringer

Publisher: James D. Blume
Executive Director, Marketing: Jeffrey Myers
Executive Director, New Business Development: Todd M. Davis
Executive Director, Sales: Ken Zagor
Director, Operations: George A. Susral
Director, Production: Douglas M. Johnston
Business Director: Jim Leonard

Vice President and General Manager: Douglas J. Guendel

Better Homes and Gardens® **Magazine**
Editor in Chief: Karol DeWulf Nickell
Senior Deputy Editor, Home Design: Oma Blaise Ford

Meredith Publishing Group
President, Publishing Group: Stephen M. Lacy
Vice President-Publishing Director: Bob Mate

Meredith Corporation
Chairman and Chief Executive Officer: William T. Kerr

In Memoriam: E. T. Meredith III (1933-2003)

CONTENTS

As an interior-design writer, I don't always travel to the locations I write about. Instead, I do my job with the aid of photographs so I can "see" more houses. This also puts me in prime position to spot trends as they emerge in the beautiful houses that are my bread and butter.

More houses, I began to notice a couple of years ago, were featuring chic, state-of-the-art, kitchens—outside. At the same time, dressy chandeliers no longer were exclusive to interiors. They were appearing on loggias, balconies—even in the middle of a grassy lawn with a sturdy tree branch for support. Decks were no longer just bland lumber, slap-dab decorated with metal furniture. They included such things as a faux-painted rug underfoot—or a real one. Or they took a soft, romantic turn with sink-down cushions, pretty pillows, and fabrics as fresh as anything found indoors.

"Outdoor rooms," in other words, were becoming a reality.

By now, most design-savvy consumers and decorating-magazine devotees are familiar with the term "outdoor room." But understanding exactly what that term means may be a different matter. It's one thing to know that outdoor rooms represent the latest frontier in home decorating; it's another to know when an umbrella table and chairs are part of an outdoor room—or when they're just an umbrella table and chairs in the yard. This book is designed to acquaint you with the ingredients that make the difference. Then, you can transform your own deck into an outdoor living room—or a kitchen or a bedroom—using the design and architectural tools presented here.

Another goal is to inspire you to stretch: Who ever said that entertaining is the only legitimate function of a patio? Why not designate and design the space as an outdoor bed-and-bath suite, if that better meets your needs or wishes? I am convinced that for each room inside the home, there exists a correlating space outdoors. By presenting you with the full range of possibilities here, hopefully your pleasure of outdoors will be broadened. And, your appreciation of life without limits.

Candace Manroe

SLEEP, PLAY, WORK

It's a perfect day—not too cool, not too warm. All of nature—from the soft music of the birds and the fragrance of new-blooming flowers, to a caressing breeze and the steady smile of the sun—conspires to keep you outdoors. You grow contemplative. Peaceful ... sleepy. These are the times you long for an outdoor nest all your own—a comfortable, cozy, private retreat, shielded from the sun and neighbors, where you can stretch out, day-dream, and if you desire, drift to sleep in the fresh air.

Fulfilling that wish doesn't require a genie in a bottle. The sanctuary of the bedroom (most people's idea of the ultimate indoor haven) is just as viable outside as inside. And the outdoor sleeping space can have as many variations—from casual to formal, spartan to decorative—as any indoor bedroom. For the most privacy and protection of your outdoor bedroom, choose a structure with a roof. A gazebo, sleeping porch, or loggia will suffice. Inside a protected structure, any style of indoor bed is appropriate. Even an opulent antique bed with a canopy dripping in silks and tapestry is feasible when protected from blowing rain. Conversely, choose a more multifunctional daybed or even a wide, well-cushioned settee or sofa, the kind of sleep/sit furniture you might use for an indoor guest room. Regardless of the type of bed you choose, must-have furnishings include sealable containers that serve as caches for linens. Stash practical plastic tubs under the bed, or store more visually appealing casegoods, such as trunks or old shipping crates, in the open. The idea is to protect your soft, beautiful linens from dust, bugs, and mildew, so they are in good condition when you want to use them.

A pergola also can find good use as an outdoor bedroom. Its widely spaced upper boards create architecture that defines the sleeping area. But even when entwined with vines, the pergola won't offer much protection from the elements. Be careful in choosing weather-resistant fabrics—or practice vigilance in maintaining less impervious linens. Building a bed into a wall as a banquette is another sleeping solution. The granite wall serves the dual purpose as the side of the bed and the architectural structure identifying the boundary of the sleeping room itself. While it offers some protection and privacy, the banquette still leaves a wide-open view of the sky for cloud- or star-gazing. A soft mattress and pillows are necessities for countering the hard stone. Except in inclement weather, linen slipcovers are durable for outdoor use (like any organic fabric, linen mildews if left wet). When soiled with garden dirt, the slipcovers can be thrown in the wash.

The most casual outdoor sleeping solution is also the most common: the hammock. Whether slung between two trees or supported by its own metal frame, a hammock is the ultimate expression of happy relaxation. To make the most of the area and define the room, accessorize with an area rug. Create visual interest with potted plants or outdoor sculpture. Appeal to the ear by stationing wind chimes or a portable fountain nearby. Hammocks and lemonade go hand-in-hand, so include a small table at your bedside for caddying refreshments and reading materials, just as you would indoors.

1) ANYONE WHO HAS EVER wanted to bask in the beauty of the garden will relate to this viewing platform. Devised to fulfill the desire for a simple, serene place to meditate and appreciate nature's bounty, the platform exemplifies the adaptive reuse: It consists of an old dock panel found washed up on a beach. The salvaged piece was lugged home and built up with tall bamboo poles to create a fantasy jungle feel. The platform is softened with bedding and topped with a canopy of woven bamboo from a home improvement store. During bug season, mosquito netting is suspended from the bamboo frame to allow for an even longer nap.

2) A STONE BENCH, built as part of a tall granite garden wall, is transformed from monastic austerity into sumptuous comfort. When softened with a foam mattress and pillows, it becomes an outdoor bed. Like a daybed, the back wall of the bench serves as one side of the sleeping berth, giving the area privacy and a sense of mystery while blocking the wind and sun. White linen bedding is sturdy but elegant. Its zen-like simplicity, coupled with the natural granite, keeps the outdoor room's emphasis on organic texture instead of pattern or color. Because the bench has no overhead protection, bedding should be taken inside when not in use to prevent mildew.

3) AN OUTDOOR SLEEPING PAVILION is one of the most romantic spaces imaginable, even in its most rustic incarnation. Almost entirely open at one side, this primitive structure is little more than a corrugated metal roof over widely spaced vertical boards. The effect is far more magical than the effort required to make it. And because the architecture is rustic, the furnishings can be too. Flea market or garage sale finds or even curbside pickups salvaged on trash day make ideal dressings for the sleeping shed. A rusted iron daybed made cushy with a soft foam mattress assumes a cottage style with the addition of floppy pastel pillows plucked from the garden. The weathered look is part of the bed's charm, eliminating the need to paint or sandblast. A pair of old white bedside tables, already chipping paint, becomes none the worse for wear stationed alongside the daybed as receptacles for books or snacks. In severe weather or blowing rain, any cotton furnishings should be taken indoors.

INSIDE OUT DECORATING OUTDOOR SPACES WITH INDOOR STYLE

THIS COLONIAL HOME'S
SLEEPING PORCH is furnished
with all the accoutrements of a
bedroom, from the iron bed to the
side table, chairs, and area rug. The
indoor furniture looks appropriate in the
outdoor space because the palette and
style are keyed to the architecture. Like
the columns, the furniture is a crisp
cottage white. The red fabric accents
the flowers blooming in the garden. The
absence of screens and front-of-house
location make this the place for a nap
rather than an overnight sleep. Most
true sleeping porches are located on
the side or back of the house and
are outfitted with a full complement
of screens.

MAKING MEMORIES

Cool night breezes, music of crickets
and cicadas, and giggling long past
bedtime from the sheer excitement
of sleeping outside—these are
the experiences a sleeping porch
can etch into a child's memory
for a lifetime.

Thankfully, a new generation of
children can experience these joys
again, as the sleeping porch
reappears following near extinction.
Before air-conditioning, a porch
outfitted with beds served as a
practical solution to escaping the
built-up heat inside the home.

When air-conditioning became
more prevalent, the sleeping porch
began to disappear—and with it, the
potential for some of life's pleasant,
peaceful moments. Today's renewed
emphasis on home has restored this
residential treasure, as porches—
and all they represent—make a
welcome comeback.

1) ESPECIALLY IN MOSQUITO COUNTRY, the most comfortable sleeping porch has screens. This space offers even more creature comforts, including ceiling and floor fans that stir up a breeze on hot summer nights when the air hangs stubbornly in the doldrums. One additional feature, matchstick shades on the windows closest to the bed, creates privacy while cutting the brightness of the sun, allowing sleepers to rest past sunrise.

2) A SLEEPING PORCH is an opportunity to make a design statement that's steeped in style and comfort. Soft, restful hues set the mood. With views from the bed to the sky, blue is a natural for linens. Stacking different sizes of pillows brings definition and alluring comfort to the bed.

CATCHING ZZZZ'S

THIS OUTDOOR BEDROOM is defined foremost by a change of flooring. Wood decking underfoot distinguishes it from the surrounding garden's path of large slat tiles, announcing that this is a room and not simply a continuation of garden. Just large enough to accommodate the basics—a hammock, small table, and pair of chairs—it has all the character of a real room. An auspicious setting, beneath the shady branches of a tree, plays a role in the space's inviting feel. Portable landscaping, pots of blooming annuals pulled into the room to add color and life, completes the pleasing ambience. The design is maintenance-free—nothing but the throw needs to be stored indoors when not in use.

INSIDE OUT DECORATING OUTDOOR SPACES WITH INDOOR STYLE

1) THIS OUTDOOR BEDROOM'S STYLE is an example of natural minimalism. When nature provides props like these trees, there's no need to accessorize further. Some handiwork is hard to improve.

2) THE JOY OF DECORATING outdoor rooms comes from the enormous latitude and flexibility these spaces afford. An outdoor bedroom can be as furnished as an indoor haven with minimal effort and expense. This hammock attains indoor style with a pile of colorful kilim, Indian, and other geometric-patterned pillows. It requires little effort, yet the area draws the eye as assertively as a more complexly decorated space.

A PRIMER ON HAMMOCKS

In addition to the two basic hammock styles, strung-to-the-tree and freestanding frame, there are two major materials categories.

Rope
•**COTTON:** This material conforms to the body for a perfect fit, and its open weave breathes to keep you cool. However, it leaves a grid pattern on the skin, discolors over time, and should be kept indoors when not in use to prevent mildew and rot.
•**POLYESTER OR OLEFIN:** This synthetic won't mildew, but it's not as comfortable as cotton. It also can be rough and it doesn't conform to the body as easily as cotton.
•**COLORED COTTON OR POLYESTER:** Choose fibers dyed before they're woven into yarn or the color will bleed onto clothing when it comes into contact with perspiration.

Fabric
•**COTTON FABRIC:** The ultimate for coolness and softness, cotton is high-maintenance. Sun and water will fade it, and moisture mildews it.
•**SINGLE-LAYER COATED POLYESTER:** Quick-drying and water-resistant, it doesn't feel as good as cotton but it will last longer.
•**QUILTED:** Increased softness counters the rough feel of the weather-resistant fabric. This style contains a center of water-resistant foam. A variety of patterns and colors is available. Flip the fabric after rain to drain water.

Care
Clean rope in the bathtub with mild detergent and a small amount of bleach. Scrub fabrics outdoors with a mild detergent; then rinse with a hose.

CATCHING ZZZ'S

1

1) INSTEAD OF THE DE RIGUEUR DECK, this area in back of the house takes the more intimate form of an all-purpose sleeping pavilion. Its couch and chaise—flea market pieces rendered more comfortable and stylish with a little ingenuity—are good for entertaining or hanging out with the family. They're also ready for a change of pace when you are. The slipcovered couch is wide enough to become a bed, while the chaise provides a second sleep space. The real attraction to this outdoor bedroom is its roll-down shades. The fabric instantly creates privacy and protects from insects, particularly important features when sleeping is the goal. The porous fabric also breathes, so the bedroom stays cool. The material is mounted on rollers—a project easy to do yourself—and the rollers are then fastened to horizontal beams at ceiling height. Decking underfoot is painted as faux area rugs in pastel shades that repeat the slipcover colors.

2) AN OUTDOOR BEDROOM
can be as small and unobtrusive as a daybed, yet as functional as a full-size room. This garden bedroom is a custom solution that's easy to replicate. It starts with a daybed, dressed with a soft foam mattress and a bank of welcoming pillows. Old doors, sans screens, are assembled around the daybed to define the area and provide the feel of a real room. The doors do more than carve out a discrete space: They serve as the frame for roll-down mosquito netting that instantly shields the area from outdoor pests. A border of blue fabric gives the canopy a finished look that coordinates with the colors of the daybed linens.

3) STITCHED TO THE MOSQUITO NETTING at the top of the canopy frame, a dust ruffle is a minor detail that adds major impact to the outdoor bedroom.

1

INSIDE OUT DECORATING OUTDOOR SPACES WITH INDOOR STYLE

2

3

3) AN ANTIQUE MARBLE-TOP TABLE that will withstand an outdoor tour of duty becomes a quaint dressing table when used in a sleeping pavilion. Accented with a mirror and a candlestick, the table's transformation is complete. Well-cushioned outdoor chairs look amply soft for the restful room.

1) OUTDOOR SLEEPING PAVILIONS extend beyond mild-climate states. Even in the Northeast, an outdoor sleeping pavilion is a dream come true. When warmer weather finally arrives after dreary months of gray skies and frigid temperatures, settling down for a snooze in the open air is that much more appealing. This sleeping structure has all the features of a bedroom indoors, including a bed, dressing table, mirror, and chairs. But it offers one ingredient the indoors can't—fresh air.

2) THE PAVILION'S BED is actually a standard camping cot plumped up with a full-size downy ruffled comforter, folded over to fit. Mounds of pillows make the cot as pleasing to look at as it is to relax on. When the seasons change, the cot can remain right where it is, while the linens go indoors.

ROOM to play

While every indoor room can be re-created outdoors, the opposite isn't true: Some outdoor rooms can exist only in the open air. Sports and game areas that require room to run and lots of air space to throw or pitch a ball and let it soar are among the most pleasurable, and inimitable, spaces the outdoors can offer. And they require only a small investment to build.

Alleys or lanes for pitching horseshoes or rolling bowling balls are easy to include in a landscape plan. Spaces for playing croquet or badminton are even easier to design. And as sports like Italy's boccie ball or France's boules catch on in America, outdoor spaces are being reconsidered even more. Beautiful gardens or blank expanses of lawn are being redesigned as the demand increases to accommodate these imported games. But the activity doesn't need a continental flavor to be fun. Even wooden decks and stone-floor terraces can satisfy the stuff of gamesmanship, with painted or stone checkerboards and oversize checkers made from old painted tins filled with sand for stability.

The burgeoning interest in outdoor playrooms isn't so much new as it is a throwback to the 19th century when the summer homes of America's wealthiest captains of industry were outfitted with everything from grass tennis courts to regulation-size polo fields. The difference these days lies more in our democratic spirit. Outdoor playrooms are no longer limited to the rich and famous; they can be the property of anyone willing to invest in the spirit of fun.

1) POTTED PLANTS nestle up to this new, sandy boccie court, integrating it into the garden until perennials and annuals can be planted along its perimeter. At regulation size, 8×60 feet, the court adds a strong linear element to the outdoor design, serving as an axis to bisect the garden or lawn.

2) BOCCIE BALL SETS are sold in two colors, green and red, and are covered in a hard, bowling-ball-like material that resists breakage. A rake for the sand, plus a smaller target ball called the pallino, are part of the essential equipment.

WHEN IN ROME... OR AT HOME

Throwing balls at a target is the oldest game known to humankind. As early as 5,000 B.C., the Egyptians played a form of boccie (also spelled bocci and bocce) using polished rocks. From Egypt the game spread to Greece around 800 B.C., and from Greece to the Roman Empire, where it thrived.

The early Romans carved coconuts and later, hard olive wood to make their boccie balls. Under Emperor Augustus, the game became the sport of Roman statesmen and rulers. Its popularity spread to all social classes, and in 1947, Italy organized the world's first boccie clubs. Next to soccer, boccie is the most popular game in the world, knowing no age or fitness restrictions.

To start the game, the first player throws a small target ball, which must land 5 feet past the center of the lane. Each player throws his ball (also called a bowl) as close to the target as possible. If a bowl displaces others already in position, that throw is disqualified.

For more rules and regulations, visit www.bocce.org/rules.html

ROOM to play

BACKYARD COURTS

Start by consulting a professional court designer (search the Internet for backyard court companies). Water is the greatest enemy of a play court, and a professional can establish the right grade to ensure water drains. Also a professional court company can determine the court surface best for you. These companies offer packages that include equipment such as basketball hoops, posts for nets, rebounders, and optional lighting. To compare pricing, ask for quotes on the most popular multipurpose court size: 35×65 feet.

Court surface options include:
•Concrete base with a water-base acrylic surface (the typical tennis court surface)
•Concrete base with a suspended polypropylene surface (vertical cushioning that's easier on the joints)
•Extra-durable all-weather acrylic surface (sturdier than a traditional tennis court)
•Prefabricated rubber mat coated with multiple layers of acrylic (looks like a standard court, but "gives" and withstands a variety of climates)

TWO OUTDOOR PLAYROOMS exist side by side in this home, dedicated to healthy family fun away from the TV and video games. A pair of brick retaining walls frames a long, narrow strip of lawn, sandy at either end, to be used as a horseshoe court. At the top of the terracing, a multipurpose court invites kickball, basketball, and any games the family invents. About half the size of a tennis court, the area consists of a 53×36-foot slab of concrete, artistically fenced and gated in a pleasing geometric shape that breaks out of the uniformly fenced box.

BOULES ANYWHERE, ANY TIME

Some call it petanque (pay-tonk) while others insist it's boules. Both terms refer to the same outdoor pitching game between two teams which dates to the late 1800s in France. The game is played by tossing or rolling boules (boolz) as close as possible to a smaller wooden ball called a cochonnet, which is tossed first to provide a target. A point is scored for each boule that is thrown closer to the target than the opposition's closest boule.

A coin toss determines who starts the game. The first player draws a circle on the ground, about 1½ feet in diameter. While standing in the circle, he or she pitches the cochonnet 6½ to 11 yards in any direction. If the toss is too short or long, the starting team is allowed two more tries before the opposition takes possession of the cochonnet.

When the target is tossed an acceptable distance, the first player then stands with both feet inside the circle and throws the first boule as close as possible to the target. Then the opposition gets a turn. Because the cochonnet is not fixed, players may try to knock it away from the other team's nearby boule. Or they may strike at the opposition's boule, to move it farther from the target. The next player is from the trailing team. Each player from that team gets a throw until one of their boules lands closer to the cochonnet than the opposition's closest boule.

If they still fail to get closer than the opposition, the leading team gets to play all their remaining boules. A second round begins with a player from the first round's winning team tossing the cochonnet, and the game is played as before. Playing as many rounds as needed, the first team to earn 13 points wins.

1) THE ONLY EQUIPMENT needed for a game of boules is two sets of steel or plastic boules (one set for each team), which cost from $30 to $100; a cochonnet (a small wooden target ball); and a tape measure for judging distances. So teams can distinguish between balls, boules come in four different styles: no-, one-, two-, or three-line patterns.

2) THE BEAUTY OF THE FRENCH GAME, boules, is that it doesn't require a special court or playing field and adapts beautifully even to the curvy paths of a well-designed garden. A wide gravel or dirt path or an expanse of lawn amid the surrounding beauty of a garden presents the ideal setting for a friendly contest. This French garden makes an appropriate playing field, while serving as a restful green zone when the game is done.

1) EVEN WHEN THE OUTDOORS has only a small patch of grass, children gravitate there at the first sign of mild weather (and often before). So when outdoors is a scene straight out of a medieval fairy tale, imagine the magical draw. This bland backyard was converted into a child's fantasyland, replete with a castle wall and watchtower. Connecting the two areas is a brick-paved patio surrounded by a lush garden full of sweet smells and colors when in full bloom. What better place for a tea party?

2) EVEN OUTSIDE THE GATE, the whimsy begins with a carved wooden rooster, a birdbath blooming with annual color, and baskets and tubs brimming with more diverse life. This is a scene neither adult nor child can help but enjoy every time they enter.

Balance requires it

Along with other duties, outdoor rooms must offer a provision for work: to be as functional and feasible as their indoor counterparts. Thanks to the laptop, this function is readily accommodated. No special office equipment is required, just a comfortable chair and a table big enough to spread out work materials. And even a table may be stretching things: People who have adapted to working outdoors will tell you their favorite chaise lounge, in a spot shielded from direct sunlight, is their ticket to productivity. An electrical outlet isn't even a "must have" when the laptop battery is fully charged.

For those employed

in fields that aren't driven by computers, outdoor work requirements are even less demanding. Sketching blueprints or fashion designs requires only a small table or portable writing desk. Painting, on the other hand, necessitates space to spread out, perhaps on a picnic-size table. Some artists prefer to work like the Impressionists, en plein air, while others prefer the protection of a partially enclosed structure such as a gazebo or outdoor pavilion. An artist's or writer's atelier in the treetops is tough to beat as a renewable source of inspiration.

Sometimes work

is an avocation. With gardening as America's number one pastime, homeowners are designing potting sheds and other outdoor rooms, nooks, or crannies especially geared to this passion.

Outdoor work rooms

appeal to all ages. More families are catching on to the idea of outdoor craft stations for their children as attractive alternatives to electronic games. Designing a craft area entails little more than finding a well-worn table and chairs that won't suffer from splattered paint or spilled ink, adding some festive decorative touches with plants or outdoor art, and including all the accoutrements of the craft. Children soon prove what parents know but sometimes forget: Work can and should be fun.

ON SMALL LOTS square footage for outdoor rooms is as precious as it is for inside spaces. There's no room to waste. That's why this outdoor office, like so many home offices, is a multipurpose space. All special equipment, including the computer, is portable so the office can become a gathering place for family and friends when the work is done. Its banquettes, table, and stool are conducive to entertaining, but they also present plenty of room for spreading out work materials. (Who wants to have a conventional computer desk outdoors anyway?)

Trays holding documents, mail, and other work or household papers keep business organized, allowing it to be conveniently transported outdoors and in. And because the mobile office entails organization, it cleans up the act for inside work, too, ensuring materials are already sorted.

Courtyards make good locations for outdoor offices because their walls serve as windbreaks, reducing the frustration posed by flying or fluttering papers. Tucking an office close to the house is an asset, too, minimizing the glare on the laptop, one of the biggest challenges in working outdoors.

Tip: A comfortable chair is as important for outdoor office work as it is indoors. Try out different styles and materials before making your selection, and don't let appearances be the only guide. (Adirondack chairs look wonderful, but they wreak havoc on the back and neck when used for work.) Consider hard metals or bare woods that can be more comfortable with padded cushions. Chairs outfitted with adjustable back cushions are desirable when you need extra lumbar support.

QUIETUDE IS ONE of the advantages a courtyard brings to an outdoor office. This carefully designed rock-walled space offers peaceful seclusion for thought, as well as a beautiful green and flowering environment for inspiring creativity. The table's location in front of the fountain, with the sensory appeal of running water, deepens the contemplative mood. The nearby cart can be enlisted to caddy work materials. Pillows and cushions can soften the chairs.

Tip: One essential for working outdoors: paperweights. Without them documents may blow away with each gust. Stack all your related papers together in wicker dinner trays, then top them with attractive rocks. When you no longer need the rocks to pin paper, they can serve as outdoor accessories.

1) AMBIENCE IS EVERYTHING in this treetop writer's retreat. Like a jungle lair or the romantic treehouse from *Swiss Family Robinson*, the space nestles high amid the trees, blanketed by a sea of green. It's easily accessible via catwalks, which at the same time imbue it with a distinct sense of privacy. The gambrel roof makes an architectural statement that visually knits the retreat to the house, and its extra depth keeps the office dry even with the walls left open.

2) THIS TIN-ROOFED GAZEBO provides a cottage-style answer to an outdoor office. Carefully but sparingly detailed with rooftop finials and corner corbels, it exudes a timeless grace, defined by its crisp, classic palette. The architecture consists of two structures: the main gazebo and a smaller storage building. The smaller structure, which is fully enclosed, serves as a safe, dry place to stash and lock up expensive office equipment when it's not being used. Like the gazebo itself, the mini building offers other interpretations: it can be used as a child's hideout, a potting shed, or a shelter for pets.

1) A PRIMITIVE TABLE, protected from the elements in a loggia, provides a spot for flower arranging and potting when not enlisted for meals. The key to this multifunction? The table's rustic finish only improves with nicks, smudges, and scrapes.

2) A WHIMSICAL PEDIMENT that's actually a birdhouse for three transforms a center-gable shed from a boring outbuilding into attractive architecture. Functioning as a potting shed, the room is accessorized in tools of the trade, with bundles of hydrangeas hanging to dry from a rail dotted with terra-cotta pots. Like any indoor space, decorating enhances the area. Here a sisal rug dresses up the wood plank floor. The practical rug hides spilled potting soil and muddy footprints. White-painted paneling brightens the walls. With a white potting table and stool and shiny copper watering cans, the room looks so attractive that the stable-style doors are kept open even when gardening is done.

3) AN OUTBUILDING isn't
essential for creating a potting area.
Any exterior wall makes a good
backdrop for a potting table. Though
tables designed specifically for potting
are available, adapt any kind of table to
assist in gardening, provided it's not too
finely finished. A marble slab on a
cast-off table makes cleanup easy and
protects the wood from warping with
exposure to rain.

1) THE MOST ESSENTIAL INGREDIENT for creating an outdoor art studio is imagination—the ability to look beyond narrow definitions of how a table and benches can function. And what better place for inspiring creativity than the beauty of a garden? The brightly colored tablecloth and pillows increase the sense of celebration that's fundamental to any artistic endeavor.

2) WITH ITS WIDE-OPEN ATTITUDE, the outdoors opens new avenues for creative projects that are especially appealing to children. Here they literally can think outside the box: Paints don't need to be confined to paper or canvas but can decorate the glass jars used for washing brushes.

1) OFFICE CONSTRUCTION is simplified by the absence of a foundation and footings. The same flooring material that covers the outlying garden paths and patio serves as the office floor.

2) THIS OUTDOOR OFFICE approaches work with a playful attitude. The window frames are sans glass, allowing the breeze to blow through and the curtains to billow. While the sheers are porous enough to admit air, they provide sufficient density to keep insects out. When the office isn't in use, the sheers pull to the opposite side of the shutters and the shutters close to protect against rain.

3) THE MOST FUNCTIONAL outdoor office is afforded by freestanding architecture. Though seemingly fully enclosed, this space also can open up completely on the front side, thanks to a wall of glass doors. And because the office has no insulation or climate control (it's used only in mild weather), leaving the wall of doors open to catch the breeze is routine. Additional air flow is provided by transoms and large windows without panes. Sheers and shutters disguise the nakedness. As a do-it-yourself project, the office is easy to build: It requires no footings and can be constructed directly on top of an existing patio floor. To create a "real room" look, a full fireplace surround decorates one wall, adding architectural presence to a bare wall. In addition to the computer desk and chair, furnishings include a comfortable recliner for taking a break, reading a book, or catching a nap.

BATHS and KITCHENS

As any backcountry camper will attest, the great outdoors has a dearth of bathing facilities. While that primitive aspect may be charming on a camping trip, it's likely a less-appealing reality when the venue is your own backyard: How much time will you really spend playing, working, and sleeping in your stylishly decorated outdoor rooms if it means you have to stay grimy in the process? After hours working in the garden, wouldn't it be nice to slip into a cool, cleansing shower before reentering the house? What if you could? Perhaps you wouldn't want to go indoors at all, opting to stretch your outdoor stay long into the evening, admiring your and nature's handiwork under a starry sky.

Enter outdoor baths, comprised primarily of showers, though tubs and whirlpools also fall into this category. When it comes to cleaning and cooling off in a hurry, nothing compares to the swift spray of water from a showerhead.

Not all homes need them equally. First in line is any waterfront property, especially one with a sandy beach. Here an outdoor shower isn't so much a luxury as a necessity because it helps you avoid tracking sand inside. Second in need is a home with active young children who harbor a talent for getting dirty. And third: a home of gardeners or others who work hard outdoors and want to clean up and cool off immediately.

The type of outdoor shower you select depends a lot on how much money you're willing to spend. A shower can be rigged without large expense wherever an outdoor spigot already is in place. Replumbing will drive up the cost. Good drainage is important. If a subterranean drainage system isn't provided, standing water will quickly make the shower space unappealing. Consult a contractor or plumber to help with drainage rather than risk doing it yourself and making mistakes. Privacy is an important issue in determining the shape of your outdoor shower. If the outdoor area is secluded, well-shielded from prying eyes or even an errant glance from passersby, a stall may not be necessary unless you desire privacy from those under your own roof. Equally viable are showers out in the open, with no privacy screening; showers totally enclosed, with a lockable door; and showers in stalls that provide complete privacy but without a door (similar to public restrooms with doorless partition entries that turn a corner for privacy).

When it's time to relax, a tub's the ticket. Outdoor bathtubs are still a rarity in America, but the ones featured here may inspire more. In contrast, whirlpools integrated into their outdoor setting with decking, comfortable seating, and attention to decorating details are one of the outdoors' most popular features. The effort it takes to decorate a whirlpool space and make it special is miniscule, especially compared to the benefits it will reap day after day, season after season.

Whether shower, tub, or whirlpool, each option makes the outdoors more user-friendly and more pleasant to enjoy.

BATHING au naturel

1) ANOTHER BRAND OF NATURAL, this hot tub tucked tidily into the ground without the distraction of decking looks more organic than synthetic. For all purposes it appears as a small pond in nature yet offers all the therapeutic and recreational functions of a whirlpool.

2) NOT FOR EVERYONE, this outdoor soaking tub is made from an old-fashioned tub and is housed in a secluded garden. Trees and shrubs in the landscaping provide a privacy screen, and the climate in California is mild enough to bathe outdoors all year long.

2

BATHING au naturel

1) RUSTICITY AND PRIVACY team up for an outdoor shower stall that looks like an extension of the woods but functions with the amenities of indoors. Three walls of barn board and a fourth "shower curtain" wall ensure privacy. An open-air arbor ceiling creates an idyllic outdoor mood with a canopy of treetops dipping into the space. More importantly, the arbor serves as an anchor for the showerhead. The garden hose runs along the arbor beams so it is inconspicuous, and the tap is turned on at the wall, providing an easy-does-it solution you can do yourself, without the expense of additional plumbing. Pulled into the stall, a garden bench provides a place to sit. Flooring is a montage of mixed materials, including leftover ceramic tiles, limestone, and brick pavers.

2) FRESHENING UP in the open air is enhanced when the accessories are as vivid as the outdoors. A collection of towels shows off its colors on the sunniest day. Rolled up and placed in an iron basket, they are not only functional but also decorative accents that add to the festive feel of the outdoor-bathing experience. The basket keeps the towels organized and clean and sits on a shelf in a protected area until needed.

1) A NARROW column of glass block prevents the adjoining stucco wall from getting wet and mildewing. The glass block also serves an aesthetic function, suggesting the glinting play of sunlight on the sea. The stall's glazed blue tile wraps around the other patio wall to continue the palette and protect that wall from moisture. Flooring in the stall is a continuation of the sandy tile used on the patio floor. A raised lip at the edge of the stall keeps water from sloshing over onto the patio.

2) A WATERFRONT HOME presents a strong need for an outdoor shower, which can be used for quick cleanups to avoid tracking sand or mud into the house or pool. The water itself serves as the inspiration for the palette, with shiny Mediterranean-blue glazed ceramic tiles that mirror the sea just yards away. Buff, the other hue in the shower stall, is the color of the beach sand. Used underfoot on larger (12×12 inches) matte-finish ceramic tiles, the mottled beige shade hides sandy footprints, keeping the tiles from looking dirty and requiring high maintenance. Because it's mainly used to wash sand off swimsuits and privacy isn't an issue, the shower stall is left open to capture the views. It is tucked into the side of a covered patio, making use of the existing architecture instead of requiring a separate structure.

1

1) **NO MATTER** where your home is, you can introduce a tropical flavor with an outdoor shower built right onto an exterior wall. This stall, which remains open and therefore requires more of a finished look, is a focal point of the landscape. A carved Bali mask is reincarnated as a humorous caddy for the showerhead, spouting a waterfall from its lips. More primitive carvings stand just beyond the stall for an integrated theme. A rectangular inset of colorful glazed tiles is cut into the background of terra-cotta tiles that defines the shower space.

2) **OPEN BEAM** construction gives this shower stall a transparent roof that lets the sunlight stream through, creating beautiful effects with light and shadow. Built onto a side of the house, much like a small portico, a shower stall like this could be added on any time after a home's construction. Its clean island style repeats the architectural design of the house itself, which featured a porthole-shaped window just around the corner from the stall. A raised garden wall filled with blooming plants abuts the house and stall, brightening both with color.

1) ONE OF THE MOST attractive hot tub spaces can be created with a custom tub built into the ground. The belowground tub leaves the landscape unimpaired, appearing not as an intrusion but as an oasis amid a desert of decking. Plus, the in-ground tub means there's no awkward climb to enter, only a smooth descent. With lounge chairs and chaises encircling it, this round pool bubbles with an invitation to kick back, relax, and soak up the moment.

2) GIVEN ITS BULK as well as its importance to entertaining, a hot tub should provide an eye-pleasing addition to the landscape, not an eyesore plunked down with no effort made to blend into the setting. Here the most effective spot for the tub lies at the far end of the garden, just beneath a low garden wall that defines the approach to the whirlpool. On the other side of the tub, a pair of classical freestanding columns suggests the ancient Roman baths and brings definition to the area without enclosing it within actual walls. A pair of cushioned outdoor chairs pulled close to the tub is important for imbuing the space with the feel of a real room. The chairs also offer a convenient respite when the water grows too warm or it's just time for a break.

DOES AN OUTDOOR HOT TUB MAKE SENSE FOR ME?

The massaging swirl of warm water on tired muscles is one of today's little perks, a compensation for the faster pace and increased stress so many people experience. While indoor whirlpool tubs are sublime, there's something alluring about a hot tub situated outdoors under an open sky. Most outdoor hot tubs are larger than their indoor counterparts, due to the extra space available outdoors. Even with a small yard or deck, space isn't usually an issue, which isn't the case indoors—most bathrooms' square footage is already used up, requiring extensive remodeling and expense to accommodate a hot tub.

Because of their larger size, outdoor hot tubs are more often flagged for recreational functions, serving as a gathering spot for friends and family after rigorously playing sports, just winding down, or celebrating any time of day or night. Come winter, hot tubs provide a soothing contrast to the chill outside, especially after a workout on the slopes or in the gym. For arthritis sufferers, as well those with muscle pain from strain or exertion, hot tubs have therapeutic value.

Beyond the initial expense (which is usually under $5,000 for a standard tub that seats six to eight), before making the plunge be sure to consider increased utility bills and maintenance. Even at low temperatures, hot tubs drive up heating bills. Like swimming pools, they require regular cleaning of both the water and the cover, which should be kept on it whenever the tub is not in use.

1) THREE LITTLE WORDS

capture the mindset and magic behind this spa: location, location, location. The in-ground whirlpool is situated at the edge of the woods, where fall's foliage provides a backdrop of amber, red, and green. Forming a border between the natural and synthetic environments is a low-slung line of rounded shrubs and various bushes. The planted border frames the corner of the spa area, and both sides of the border converge, mirroring the point on the teardrop-shaped hot tub. Natural slate in irregular shapes forms the flooring, and comfortable cushioned chaises and lounge chairs furnish the sitting area.

2) AN ALTERNATIVE to a

freestanding spa is a hot tub built onto the side of the swimming pool. A wall divides the two structures to keep the warmer and cooler water from diluting each other. The all-inclusive treatment shown here still acknowledges the need for the "spa room" to be outfitted with furniture for frequent breaks from the tub. An outdoor dining table and chairs offer just the ticket.

Tip: Although spas need covers when not in use, it's a good idea to consider the proximity of potted plants and the mess they might present if tipped over. Also avoid planting any berry-producing shrubs or trees near the tub. They can stain the surface, besides being difficult to clean up. Locate the tub away from mature trees—deciduous trees' leaves will quickly fill up the tub come fall, and evergreen needles can be downright painful.

No outdoor room has grown more in sophisticated amenities and appearance than the kitchen. In the 19th century, outdoor summer kitchens were fixtures of stately Southern homes. The summer kitchen, situated in a separate building behind the house, was a solution for preparing meals while keeping the main house from growing unbearably hot.

Now fast-forward to post-World War II, to all regions of America and homeowners of all income levels. It was then, when the GIs returned from overseas, that the barbecue grill began drawing families outdoors for informal gatherings that celebrated companionship, mild weather, and the unbeatable taste of food hot off the grill. Patios soon entered the vocabulary of homes' floor plans, and picnic tables, which had been mainly the domain of parks, began sprouting up in backyards.

Much has changed. Today's outdoor kitchen, while an evolution of both the summer kitchens of old and 1950s backyard patios with barbecue grills, is far more than both. The 21st-century take on outdoor kitchens includes, like old summer kitchens, a well-stocked, full-service facility with space for food preparation, cooking, cleanup, and storage. More often than not, they're integrated into existing outdoor spaces as extensions of a deck, patio, or poolside area. While not fully enclosed, the kitchens often are tucked under an overhang or built inside an open-sided pavilion, so there is some protection from the elements. Other kitchens sidle up to the pool as a freestanding island constructed of weather-tolerant natural materials. And still others are cleverly wrapped beneath the stairwell leading from one outdoor elevation to another. Every situation, every home, and every homeowner's needs and wants vary greatly.

Countertop materials range from slate, granite, or ceramic tile, to one-of-a-kind pottery-shard mosaics from a collection of damaged keepsake china. Weather-impervious woods such as teak and redwood can withstand rain and snow as cabinetry in an exposed kitchen, but usually outdoor kitchens that have finished cabinets include some provision for shelter, such as a pavilion or loggia roof.

Short of a full-fledged kitchen with a dishwasher, refrigerator, sink, and ample counter space, the newest offerings in outdoor grills provide many of the options needed to allow the outdoors to serve a kitchen function. The new gas grills, like their indoor counterparts, are state-of-the-art. They come in sleek stainless steel, by makers such as Viking and Vieluxe, and feature not only a traditional grill but side-unit stovetops with multiple gas burners. (More burners are available with larger grills.) More expensive models include an additional built-in work space. Portable furniture, such as carts on casters, can fill in the storage function or serve as temporary work areas.

1) FABULOUS VIEWS make this backyard deck a favorite destination for the entire family. An outdoor kitchen only enhances the enjoyment. The kitchen utilizes existing space by being tucked under the stairwell, where the steps from an upper terrace descend to a deck and on to a step-down patio.

Tip: Keep your outdoor kitchen neutral for the most natural look, but provide interest with a single accent color. Even if your kitchen is portable and it isn't realistic to introduce color in an architectural element such as counter or backsplash tiles, there's still plenty of opportunity. Use an accent color or even a palette of jazzy hues in colorful plastic glassware, silverware, and napkins.

2) THE ENTIRE KITCHEN—
refrigerator, stove, storage, and all—is
only as tall as standard counters. That's
a plus for a family with small children.
They can easily access the refrigerator
when thirsty, and help themselves to a
snack when hungry. The island unit is
made of stucco, instead of wood, to
merge with the house and withstand the
weather. Countertops are a subtle
natural stone that blends with the
slate-tile flooring. Ceramic tiles on a
small-lipped backsplash and on the
stucco provide decorative accents.

3) BLUE AND BUFF TILES
alternate on the upper and lower rows
of a buff-tiled fireplace to frame the
area and make it a focal point. A
wrought-iron firescreen adds custom
detailing and consistency to the
kitchen's design—the same wrought-
iron design covers the storage cabinets.

1) EASILY ACCESSIBLE FROM THE HOUSE, the kitchen pavilion is situated steps off the back deck. Its roofline hits just below the eaves of the rear of the house, low enough not to compete with the gable of the house's dormer. Only one side of the pavilion—with the kitchen counters and cook area—is walled. To visually connect the pavilion to the rest of the house, the lower half of the exterior of the wall continues the white-painted wood of the deck's railing, the garage, and the wood trim on the house.

2) LIKE THE SUMMER KITCHENS OF THE 19TH CENTURY, this outdoor kitchen stands on its own. Unlike those antecedents, it has a modern airiness. Open at three sides, the pavilion welcomes fresh air and views while offering overhead protection from precipitation. Because it's freestanding, it has a strong identity and it needs no decorative sleights of hand to give it definition or integrate it into a setting. Its boundaries are crisply articulated by a pitched roof. Exposed beams add charm inside, and dark-stained pine flooring announces a break from the grassy meadow. Structural pillars supporting the pavilion curve at the top, arching to a point at the ceiling's peak. Because of the protected roof, treated pine cabinets are in no danger of rot. The feel of the pavilion is light and breezy—white is the only accent color; the rest is natural wood. White wall lamps throw light down to the working surfaces while picking up the white of the ceiling and metal patio furniture.

1) A CABANA is another option for an outdoor kitchen. This one is enclosed on three sides, and a pair of floor-to-roof lattice panels frames the entry on the open front side. In wet or cold climates, it is a most practical solution, offering protection from the elements while maintaining an open-air spirit. Not only are appliances, cabinetry, and countertops protected, but so are furnishings. That means a larger pool of furniture to choose from, including pieces not specially made for outdoors. A grid of stepping stones edged with grass naturalizes the area in between the pavilion and the pool, a beautiful option to covering the poolside entirely with decking, tiles, or any other hard, contiguous surface.

2) A NATURAL GATHERING SPOT, the cabana kitchen is designed with many purposes in mind. A large square cocktail table defines a space intended for both conversation and casual dining, with a rattan chair and a comfortable upholstered love seat pulled up close. Additional dining space is provided on the other side of the kitchen work counter, at a bar furnished with cane-and-bamboo barstools. Should anyone grow weary, a cat nap or even a long night's sleep is enabled by the love seat, which unfolds.

3) FOR A SMALL STRUCTURE, the cabana is packed with architectural interest including a fan light and a wood ceiling with exposed beams. A bar on the back wall behind the kitchen work counter is defined by a horizontal strip of thick molding. Two vertical rows of built-in shelves flank a space-enhancing center mirror. Stemware is stored on a couple of the small shelves; collectibles displayed on other shelves personalize the kitchen.

4) THE CABANA'S SHAKER-STYLE CABINETS repeat the clean white beach-house look of the lattice exterior which is simple and charming. Because the cabinets are protected, they can be crafted of an untreated wood, like an indoor model. Low maintenance was considered equally with appearance in choosing materials and finishes. Earthy tile countertops are easy to clean and affordable. Painted gray, the wood floor is user-friendly, forgiving of dust, dirt, and wet tracks from the pool.

1) A PERGOLA IS ONE OF THE MOST architecturally interesting outdoor structures and also one of the simplest to construct. It is little more than a sturdy frame topped with an airy grid of boards laid on the diagonal. But the look is only half the secret to this kitchen's success. The other half is location. Just feet away from a back corner of the house, the outdoor kitchen is contained in the niche between the house and a garden wall, tucked off the main-axis approach that steps up to the back door. That out-of-the-way location fits perfectly between two outdoor elements, giving the kitchen the definition of a real room in a uniquely outdoors way. The cooking area is at the back of the kitchen, in front of a grid-wood wall that repeats the theme of the pergola's ceiling in a smaller square motif.

2) **ALTHOUGH THE PERGOLA KITCHEN** is tucked off the approach to the house's back entry, it forms one end of a second major axis (a straight line defining the landscape plan) that terminates in the swimming pool. This means that the kitchen's orientation is toward the pool, encouraging a back-and-forth flow between the two spaces, similar to that of a kitchen and living area within an open great room.

3) **A STUCCO FIREPLACE** with a slate-trimmed firebox is the kitchen's focal point. Overhead pine beams radiating out from the top of the fireplace like shafts of sunlight draw the eye toward the hearth. Smart space planning positions the stove adjacent to the fireplace, while on the other side, a built-in bench provides seating close to the warmth. The dining table is arranged directly in front of the fireplace, overlooking the pool at the opposite end.

1

1) SHINY BLUE GLAZED CERAMIC TILES make a sparkling statement across this outdoor kitchen's countertops and backsplash. Domed architecture open on one side has the feel of an open-air room with the protection of an enclosed building. It features blond horizontal wood boards rising up to the ceiling, accented with painted vertical beams that repeat the blue of the tiles. Plenty of storage awaits in both hung and floor cabinets. This scheme has all the traditional indoor kitchen amenities, including a dishwasher.

2) AS WIDE-OPEN AS ALL OUTDOORS, the outdoor kitchen is open to liberties with palette and design that might be considered risky indoors. This mosaic tile countertop is a case in point, drawing from myriad colors and shapes that say "fun"—exactly what the owners wanted to communicate with this alternative kitchen. The tile-topped island counter is a work and storage area plus an eating and serving space.

3) A BROWN ROPE MOTIF TRIMS the edge of the countertop, and garden greenery reaches nearly to the top of the counter, integrating it into the outdoor landscape.

1) **THIS TOP-OF-THE-LINE GRILL** includes side burners for stovetop cooking and an infrared heat source for roasting, in addition to a full-size grill.

2) **COUNTERTOP BURNERS** can slide into an outdoor structure for a custom look.

3) **A PORTABLE STAINLESS-STEEL** serving cart from Vieluxe enables an outdoor grill space to become a full-service kitchen.

4) **THE GRILL STILL IS KING** in this outdoor kitchen, which is defined by a low, brick-topped horseshoe-shaped wall. The grill is situated inside the wall; on the opposite side, the wall is an all-in-one working, serving, and dining counter big enough to accommodate a buffet with room left for stylish presentation.

KITCHENS TO GO

Permanent outdoor kitchens in special structures are indisputably deluxe, but are by no means the only route to outfitting this special room. Portability remains the operative word for most people to realize their dream of an outdoor kitchen.

Because outdoor rooms are now a strong growth industry, more products are available than ever before. Grills from high-end stove manufacturers, such as Viking, rival the offerings for indoor appliances. Carts on casters provide work and serving space. Task lighting is enabled by weatherproof floor lamps or sconces that are easier on the eye than harsh outdoor floodlights. Small, dorm-size refrigerators tuck out of sight under a table or bench skirted with a weatherproof cloth.

Colorful, nonbreakable tableware earmarked for outdoor use adds a festive feel to alfresco dining. You can store fabric items in airtight tubs that slide underneath an outdoor coffee table, or skirt the plastic tubs themselves to create instant tables.

Another option is to find a handy storage space inside the house especially for outdoor products. The only function not provided in these kitchens-to-go is cleanup: Unless you're using disposable products, you'll still need to step inside to wash utensils and dinnerware in the sink and dishwasher—but not until the party's over!

1) A ROLL-DOWN GARAGE-STYLE DOOR keeps this waterfront kitchen sealed off from the salt breeze when not in use. The kitchen comes with all the perks of indoor living, but with minimal hassle. A sink, dishwasher, stove, compact refrigerator, and work space are provided along and below one long counter. Dish storage, seasonings, and even the microwave are above the counter on adjustable shelves that can be lowered, heightened, or expanded to accommodate small appliances, foods, or decorative collectibles. Only the kitchen, which really is just a long, narrow shed, can be enclosed. Eating areas are in the open air. A dining table is a few feet away on the patio and a counter bar overlooking the ocean provides additional eating space.

2) ANOTHER LONG, LEAN KITCHEN, with the protection of an indoor space and the open-air ease of an outdoor room, is attainable with a set of folding glass doors. The idea is to build a kitchen island that is a single counter area for all cooking, storage, work, and cleanup. The structure is enclosed at the back and at both ends. The front is glassed in with bifold doors that can be entirely opened or closed for a best-of-both-worlds experience.

INSIDE OUT DECORATING OUTDOOR SPACES WITH INDOOR STYLE

1) **A NATURAL EXTENSION** of its environment, this river-rock kitchen island continues the cobblestone motif and construction used throughout the home's landscaping, from its towering outdoor fireplace to its garden walls. Pushed away from the central conversation area, the kitchen island is bordered at the rear by the tall garden wall, which encompasses the whole outdoor living space. Preparation and serving areas flank the grill, which is built into the island.

2) **THERE'S MORE THAN ONE WAY** to blend an outdoor kitchen into its environment. This brick kitchen, unlike the river-rock island, finds its niche by tucking into the garden walls instead of standing out in the open. Fitted flush with the extra-thick garden walls, the wine-bar section of the kitchen leaves the space looking clean. A custom touch is a mural painted above the low refrigerators and counter.

3) **THE BEAUTY OF THIS OUTDOOR KITCHEN** lies in how it meanders along the garden wall, appearing in sections. The cleanup station is housed under an arch, where a sink big enough to accommodate a pasta cooker makes cleaning up easy. The back of the station continues the mural theme of the wine-bar area, but with its own design.

4) **EVEN THE COOKING AREA** is contained within its own outdoor niche. The outdoor-worthy gas burner helps make it easy to prepare the entire meal outdoors.

LIVING and DINING

INSIDE OUT DECORATING OUTDOOR SPACES WITH INDOOR STYLE

Understanding

what constitutes an outdoor room requires thinking inside the box—that is, think first about the elements that make an indoor space a room. Only then can you apply the idea outdoors. One component high on the list of an indoor room's essential functions is the space's ability to be used any time, night or day. It makes sense that the same definition holds true for an outdoor space if that area is intended to fully serve as a room and not just another part of the lawn or landscape that's used sporadically and for limited purposes. To be a real room, an outdoor area must function at dusk or at night as well as it does during the day.

Performing

a comparable function is, however, the extent to which an outdoor room strictly matches its indoor counterpart. An outdoor rooms at night is about mood and mystery more than it is any precise, task-oriented function, such as watching TV or playing a board game. By night, outdoor living and dining spaces are intentionally compelling, quiet rooms where conversation or good dining has more importance than being able to read the fine print. Low-level lighting in outdoor living rooms not only is sufficient, it's also preferred—whereas indoors, that may not be the case at all. Outdoor spaces become "rooms" when illuminated by the soft flicker of candlelight, lanterns, torches, or a fire in the outdoor fireplace.

Outdoor rooms may,

however, be fully illuminated at night. New outdoor lamps that are weatherproof and weighted mean outdoor rooms can turn into cozy spots for reading at night, even if reading isn't the primary function. The outdoor room, above all, is prized as a romantic destination come nightfall, and its lighting most often reflects that.

1) **A BLAZING FIRE IN A PATIO FIREPLACE** denotes one of the most appealing, alluring aspects of all outdoor living. When a fine meal is part of the hearthside package, the experience becomes the stuff of memories with warmth, wood smoke, and delicious flavors all melding together to etch impressions in the mind. This fireside dining room, however, doesn't rely solely on the hearth blaze for illumination. Suspended from a wood beam supporting the pergola's stick ceiling, a pair of wrought-iron lanterns lends a golden glow to the table underneath. The electric light fixtures, though perhaps not as romantic as candlelight, make the space usable even in the stiffest breeze.

2) **WHEN A ROARING OUTDOOR FIRE** isn't an option, candles come in a close second, making outdoor rooms inhabitable and alluring after nightfall. When entertaining begins during the day, anticipate the hours ahead by including candles in the tabletop arrangements. This fete cranks up in the late afternoon and promises to last long into the night, thanks to thoughtful planning that included hurricane lamps among the essential party fare.

GOOD by night

Tip: For outdoor use, try hanging a hurricane lamp over your table. It creates the feel of an indoor dining room and is less likely to be extinguished by a breeze than a candle chandelier.

INSIDE OUT DECORATING OUTDOOR SPACES WITH INDOOR STYLE

1) A TABLE AND CHAIRS PLACED on the lawn can be lackluster. But go one small step further with overhead lighting and suddenly the space is more than a scrap of furnished lawn; it now has the essence of an outdoor room. Special wiring for electrical fixtures isn't necessary. The same effect is achievable using a candle chandelier or, as shown here, a hanging hurricane lamp.

2 & 3) MYSTIQUE is what this outdoor dining room is all about, in no small part due to the parade of candles that light it in contrast to its surroundings. A warm glow peeks through the lattice walls, making the room enticing from a distance. Up close, the effect is just as compelling. A variety of candles from pillars to tapers, placed at varying heights from the ground up, sweep the eye across the space in a dancelike rhythm.

GOOD by night

THIS OUTDOOR LIVING ROOM shows at its best at night, when it's revealed as a series of seductive chambers stepping up to entertaining. Lighting is the key. Instead of a single light source, the space has many different types placed at various heights. Solar ground lights charged by the sun during the day illuminate the conversation area at night, outlining the ground along one perimeter. A candelabra on a side table draws the eye up midway, while an assortment of candles in sconces, in pots, and on plates urges attention to the top of the fence that is the room's back boundary. The lighting continues to the next level in hanging lanterns suspended at different heights. Up one more step, a third conversation area is lit in strands of lights that swag down vertically, adding a sculptural shape to the design's dynamic.

As outdoor dining

becomes an art, it's evolving from burgers served on a picnic table covered with a plaid, plastic cloth. While casual outdoor feasting still commands a place in homes and hearts, more options present themselves for an alfresco fete. In nearly all areas of outdoor entertaining, the scales have tipped on the side of sophistication, following consumers' overall elevated tastes. For outdoors this means the dining furniture, dinnerware, ambience, and food can be as elegant, colorful, complex—or just plain fun—as anything cooked inside. And as for the fun, outdoor dining rooms have an edge over indoor spaces.

Creating an

outdoor dining room is about more than finding an attractive table and four chairs. First analyze your needs. What is it you want from a dining room outdoors? An intimate spot where a twosome can gather for late-night glass of wine or a mid-morning brunch? A cheerful place for entertaining a crowd? Something in between? When will you use the space—primarily during the day or night, in summer only, or all year long? Do you anticipate expanding the dining area with an outdoor kitchen at some point?

Decide what size space

works best to meet those needs, and where the space would best be located. For an intimate dining area, a tuck-in table close to a private part of the house is a good choice, but so is a table-for-two hidden deep in the lawn. For large-scale entertaining, a bigger area obviously is required—one that accommodates a long banquet table and perhaps a couple of smaller tables as well. Built-in bars are another option. If you want to use your outdoor dining room during chilly weather, investigate building a fireplace, or consider a freestanding style. Heat lamps and ceiling fans are other heating options. A chandelier above the dining table is a lovely element, and although small, it requires planning the space to include some type of ceiling, arbor, or pergola for mounting the fixture. Decisions on function, however, must come first.

With the big questions

out of the way, concentrate on style. Continue the decorating style of the interior to your outdoor dining room. Of course, there are exceptions, but generally it's true that a richly traditional home, for example, presents too disturbing a contrast when teamed with a stark, contemporary outdoor dining room. Also if the outdoor dining room is close to the house, choose a palette compatible with the exterior and interior of the home so the visual transition between the spaces is smooth.

A commonsense

adherence to basic design principles doesn't mean you should always let rules rule. Even if your home is an all-white cottage country design, your dining room outdoors can readily indulge the choice of colorful quilts and floral fabrics. If your interior is lean modern but you desire a rustic approach to the style outside, feel free to follow your heart. Keeping the palette low-key and neutral can be enough to tie the rustic dining room back to the house's contemporary design.

Whether the dining room

is sheltered or in the open can make a difference in the kinds of fabrics, centerpieces, and dinnerware you choose. Organic fabrics can be left outside in a sheltered space without threat of mildew. But many homeowners enjoy taking their finest tableware outdoors for each occasion, then storing it back indoors. So except for items so fragile they might be broken in a breeze, there really are no restrictions in what can be used outdoors. If anything, the outdoor dining room offers more freedom of choice. Mixing bright colors of glassware and silverware that might be viewed as garish indoors can be done outdoors with aplomb.

INSIDE OUT DECORATING OUTDOOR SPACES WITH INDOOR STYLE

1) A DINING AREA away from the house, deep in the woods, can have a rustic ambience all its own not contingent on the design of the house. Visually, this dining room is connected to other features in the landscape: The pedimented frame of the religious carving that defines one corner of the room is the same shade of forest green as the footbridge, and the paler green dining chairs pick up softer shades of green from the trees. The result is a room that serenely, almost secretively, blends into its environment. The "ceiling" of the space is a big tree branch. It not only shades the area, but serves as a place to hang a lantern over the table. The brick-paver flooring brings more definition to the room, distinguishing the space from the outdoors around it.

2) ANOTHER ROUTE to a rustic outdoor dining room is a gazebo made with four tall tree trunks as its corner structural supports. A relatively easy do-it-yourself project, the gazebo is easily designed with roof, deck flooring, and open-wood railings. Just large enough for a small table with chairs, this structure is sited in the midst of garden and woodland, a quiet retreat for enjoying a cup of tea or coffee at the start of the day.

alFresco DINING

1) THIS DAMASK-DRESSED TABLE for two is only a step away from the master bedroom suite. The small breakfast room is defined by an arbor overhead and stone flooring underfoot. Its walls include the back of the house and garden plantings on the other three sides. Intended to blend inconspicuously with the rest of the house because of its close proximity, the room features tall yellow metal chairs and yellow candles that repeat the palette of the main house. The luscious cinnamon-colored fringed cloth matches the hue of the formal box planters that separate the room from the garden beyond.

2) A FRONT PORCH DECKED OUT for brunch can offer the same feeling of escape as a quaint bed and breakfast, minus the travel and expense. Decorating is the important factor in the success of this particular porch. Paint on the outdoor dining chairs exactly matches the trim on the house exterior. The floor boards are color-coordinated and softened with an area rug in pretty pastels. A splashy pink hydrangea freshly cut from the garden adds a finishing touch of beauty.

3) A ROOM WITH A VIEW is the central concept of this small outdoor dining area. A little marble-top table and ornately turned iron chairs need nothing more than the spectacular garden views as their raison d'être. The brick-paved terrace floor continues beyond the intimate table, not clearly defining it as a space apart. A pair of trees, however, does the trick, flanking and shading the table more romantically than walls.

INSIDE OUT DECORATING OUTDOOR SPACES WITH INDOOR STYLE

1) THE ARCHITECTURAL GRANDEUR of this stucco fireplace wall, replete with artichoke finials at the sides, highlights a dramatic outdoor dining room even before the table and chairs are positioned. To create the formal villa feel, two rows of large terra-cotta pots of pruned shrubs extend from the pool to the fireplace, defining the area in between as the dining space. Water jets on both sides of the pool spurt overlapping sprays of water in great arcs through the air to intensify the room's drama.

2) ALLOWING the architecture to make the strongest statement, the furniture takes a lower profile. Comfort is its most compelling feature—with a thick cushion on each chair. The armed end chairs also include a cushioned back to encourage longer hours lingering over a meal and conversation. Even though they cater to comfort, all parts of the chairs, including the metal frames and upholstery fabrics, are water-resistant and easy to maintain. The glass tabletop requires only a wipe down after meals. The easy-does-it concept extends to the flooring: A mosaic pattern in tiles underscores the room's Mediterranean design, and it also offers the look of an area rug without the upkeep.

3) A SIMPLE GARDEN WALL becomes an architectural focal point for this outdoor dining room. The dining space is defined by a pair of tall classical columns set close to the wall, then crowned with a weathered crossbeam and salvaged corbel accents. With the table centered in front of them, the columns establish the width of the dining area as effectively as walls. To ensure maximum attention is paid to the columns, a plaster plaque is centered in between them on the garden wall. The symmetry balances the entire dining space, while suggesting the architectural style of an Italian villa.

1) INSTEAD OF WAITING in line or reserving a table at a restaurant to celebrate Mother's Day, consider a day at home. This outdoor dining table is adorned with pretty colors and flowers for the best kind of Mother's Day brunch—the kind where somebody else does all the work.

2) FEMININE PINK PLAID instantly dresses up and softens rustic outdoor wooden dining chairs, providing inspiration for the pastel palette of the tabletop. For special occasions, consider using favorite antique quilts, bedspreads, or natural-fiber tablecloths to tame the outdoors, then bring them back indoors for safekeeping when the event is over.

3) THE SOFT COTTAGE STYLE of the outdoor dining room works with this home's vintage architecture and its light, subtle palette. This is especially important given the outdoor room's proximity to the house and the fact that a view of the outdoor dining area is embraced by the windows indoors.

OUTDOOR DINING reaches new heights of romance in an airy iron gazebo swagged in mosquito netting. Today's increased popularity of outdoor living means most home improvement stores, as well as many mail-order home and garden catalogs, offer some varieties of these portable, affordable gazebos. Placed directly on the lawn, they create an outdoor room in an instant. Or put down some patio flooring material, such as this gravel bed, to give the structure a more permanent look. Enough yard space is the only necessity before setting up this outdoor room; attractive landscaping in the background is a bonus.

INSIDE OUT DECORATING OUTDOOR SPACES WITH INDOOR STYLE

1) ADDING AN ARBOR to extend a home's roofline over a patio or deck is an easy way to create an outdoor dining room. Covered in wisteria, this arbor introduces a romantic theme that repeats itself at the table's puddling white skirt and wicker chairs. Because an open-air arbor doesn't protect against rain or wind, however, the skirts must be taken indoors or stored in a waterproof container when not in use. A folk-art ship's figurehead "flies" to one side of the table, just as a painting or sculpture would accent an indoor dining room. A plethora of plants—on the wall, in planters, and hanging in baskets—finishes accessorizing the space.

2) WHEN AN EXISTING PATIO offers more space than is needed for dining, a "divide and conquer" approach may provide an answer. This patio was too big for the desired feeling of intimacy to preside at mealtimes, but adding a small pergola changed that. Matching the dimensions of the table with only a little room to spare, the pergola carves out a dining niche that appears, and feels, apart from the rest of the patio. Sprawling vines across the top of the pergola further define the dining area.

alFresco DINING

1) **WHEN IS A DECK** furnished with a table and chairs just an ordinary deck, and when is it an outdoor dining room? This deck pleads the case for room-worthiness by matching the dining furniture with a larger group of living room furniture to denote the difference. The white wicker table and four fanback wicker chairs might look like standard deck fare, if not for the wicker settee and coffee table just around the corner. The presence of the additional pieces suggests two different functions for two different rooms. Ironically it's the creation of the outdoor living space that provides reality for the outdoor dining room. Also important are the lattice awnings overhead and the railings around the deck. One acts as a ceiling, and the other as walls, yet neither encloses the space. The umbrella's position as a freestanding element, unattached to the table, anchors the dining area and separates it from the living space.

2) THE MIX of furniture styles gives this dining table and seating the character of a real room. If used without chairs, the pair of long benches matching the table would suggest a picnic table more than a "room." When the two upholstered chairs are pulled up to the ends of the table, the area gains the presence of a room.

3) ACCESSORIES, in conjunction with a step-down elevation, transform this patio with its outdoor dining table and chairs into an outdoor dining room. The discrete level, two steps down from the pool area, suggests the arrival to a separate room. And on the table, the tall candles and smaller terra-cotta pots as a centerpiece create the decorated look.

alFresco DINING

1) WITH PRIVACY ENSURED, courtyards make wonderful outdoor dining rooms. Painted white, this Mexican table and its chairs relate to the courtyard's white architecture, integrating them into the setting. Like the walls of any room inside, the courtyard's walls receive visual interest through attention to color, texture, and shapely plants and flowers. Small art objects ensure a pleasing view in every direction.

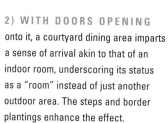

2) WITH DOORS OPENING onto it, a courtyard dining area imparts a sense of arrival akin to that of an indoor room, underscoring its status as a "room" instead of just another outdoor area. The steps and border plantings enhance the effect.

3) WELL-LANDSCAPED COURTYARDS like this offer charms that indoor dining rooms can imitate but can't replicate, such as gurgling fountains, leafy palms, and climbing vines. The arrangement of the table and chairs directly in front of the fountain, centered in the courtyard, is important to the establishment of the space's room-like feel.

Comfort is the first key

to creating outdoor rooms where the living is as easy as it is indoors. How do you know if your outdoor space is a real living room, instead of just another partially furnished patch of lawn or sparsely dressed deck or patio? Here's the infallibility test: Does the furniture feel as good to the body as it looks to the eye? It must. Anything less fails the test.

In this comfort-conscious

outdoor hangout, there is a place for a bare-wood bench or chair. Unadorned, an Adirondack chair provides the accent needed to enhance aesthetics, much like a Shaker chair brings clean-lined relief to indoor decor. But you would never consider dressing your indoor family room's conversation area in nothing but stiff, unupholstered wood furniture. So why give pause to such thoughts for outdoors? The offense is every bit as outrageous. Imagine: Friends come over to share an evening of alfresco dining, then kick back to relax as the sun sets—on brutally uncomfortable outdoor furniture.

Soften up.

Flesh out wood, metal, and hard vinyl outdoor seating with plump cushions and pillows. Choices include an increasing selection of new, weather-resistant materials in colors and patterns more attractive than the crinkly vinyl awning stripes that dominated the market just over a decade ago. Look for fabrics that breathe and wick off water to avoid mildew. Also consider using finer fabrics on pillows and cushions outdoors, then storing them in covered bins or other easily accessible caches. For modern, all-weather furnishings, don't make a purchase without trying metal mesh chairs that conform to the contours of the body for an ergonomic—and blissful—fit. Once you've got the right seat, think about the feet. You can make living easy with ottomans and footstools. Or position a coffee table in front of a settee or glider. Propping your feet up is another measure of comfort, just as essential outdoors as in.

Make it function.

Beyond the tactile, comfort translates as smooth function: having life's little pleasures at fingertips' reach. Arrange outdoor living areas using the principles of interior design. Place seating close enough for easy conversation but not so close as to invade personal space. Make groupings inviting by opening them up—no chair or settee backs facing the entrance of the space. Ensure good traffic flow by anticipating the most direct traffic lanes from one outdoor room to another, and also to indoors, keeping the lanes clear of furniture.

Ease the eye.

A final ingredient of easy living is visual appeal. An outdoor living room should be pleasing to the eye. Imbue the space with art and accessories (don't forget the obvious: green plants and fresh cuttings from the garden) for hours of pleasure.

②

1) A PARTIALLY SHELTERED
BALCONY with a gorgeous stone
wall as its backdrop is an outdoor living
room begging for design. This space
transitions from indoors to out with
hardly a ripple. The furniture is stylishly
modern and has all the cushiony feel of
an interior collection: Each chair rivals
any indoor counterpart for simply feeling
good, soft, and supportive. The teak

wood is impervious to moisture, as is
the khaki-colored synthetic upholstery
fabric. Upholstered footstools invite
propping up your feet, while a small tile-
topped table is close at hand for resting
drinks or books. There's even a display
of objets d'art on a modern shelf unit
flush with the exterior wall, to please
the eye in all directions.

2) A GRACEFUL WROUGHT-
IRON RAIL frames the wooded vista
beyond the balcony. Potted plants are
the ideal decorative accessories,
dressing up the outdoor room while
soaking up the sunshine.

①

②

1) FRIENDLY FURNITURE ARRANGEMENTS are essential to easy living outdoors, just as they are inside the home. This small outdoor living room brings guests together with a tight furniture arrangement that has two matching metal chairs facing off on either side of a small settee. Cushions amply soften the metal pieces. A coffee table in the middle knits the three seating pieces together, and side tables at either end of the settee provide additional space for setting food or glasses. The space anticipates use after dark: A weather-resistant outdoor lamp on one end table illuminates the grouping as a whole and, for those seated closest to it, permits reading after dusk—exactly what you'd expect of a room for living.

4) THIS FURNITURE ARRANGEMENT follows the great-room concept, providing multiple functions within a single open space. The dining area is closest to the fireplace for the most intimacy. The table also is strategically placed beneath two ceiling fans for equal comfort when the weather's warm. Kitchen storage surrounds the table, and a few feet beyond the dining area, a comfortable conversation grouping faces the fire. Guests can linger at the table or dawdle in the chairs paired nearby, while staying close enough to interact with anyone, anywhere in the entire space.

2) LIVING THE EASY LIFE OUTDOORS means taking advantage of every asset. At this hilltop home, that's no great challenge—the patio is dressed with an outdoor fireplace and is surrounded by incredible vistas of the city below. Thick-cushioned metal outdoor furniture is perfectly positioned to snuggle up close to the fire and to overlook the city at the same time.

3) FINDING THE RIGHT LOCATION for your outdoor conversation area involves more than simply relegating it to a patio or deck. The exact location makes a difference, just as it does inside. For a cozy setting, use an exterior wall of the house as a backdrop. Scoot furniture up close to the wall, as you would use an interior wall to place pieces. And, just as you would not want all furnishings to march along the wall inside, angle pieces out from the wall to create a friendly, circular arrangement like this. The open circle invites people in, while the back wall anchors the arrangement. Pillows soften the furnishings for an even warmer welcome.

1) ALONG WITH A PATRIOTIC THEME, "the world at your fingertips" is the design principle at work in this porch, a living room meant to be used for more than an occasional breather outdoors. The furniture is comfortable and companionably arranged. Blankets, pillows, and footstools sit ready, if needed. A marble-top Victorian side table is big enough for a reading lamp, decorative accessories, and refreshments. (Because of the porch's roof and protected enclosure, worrying about the weather wasn't an issue in the furniture selection.) Even the coffee table holds a chess game waiting to be played. Should a little privacy be preferred, white cotton curtains can be drawn closed.

2) MAKING LIFE EASY IN AN OUTDOOR ROOM can be as simple as remembering to include a lamp. Weighted with rocks and wired, a 1920s vase becomes a sturdy lamp base. This one-of-a-kind light reflects personal collecting tastes—proof that outdoor rooms hold just as much interest as those inside. The glass top over the terra-cotta table is about ease too—watermarks wipe right up.

1) **STORAGE IS** as important as aesthetics in determining how a room feels and functions. Outdoor living areas don't look any better with disarray and clutter than do their indoor counterparts. Nor is an outdoor room exactly a comfortable place for spending extended periods of time if objects that might be used there are inaccessible. This old painted cabinet solves the storage problem while contributing to the porch's good looks. It hides reading materials, comfy slippers, vases, and pots—all "vitals" for time on the porch. Covering the cabinet's door panels in a favorite wallpaper or fabric keeps the contents private and enhances the appearance.

2) **BUILT-IN SHELVES** substitute for furniture, providing storage for accessories and necessities. The small bench tucks in neatly beneath the shelves for more storage space.

3) **A WHIMSICAL** old end table painted white, with a colorful scene on top, stores such smaller items as terra-cotta pots and watering cans, while adding a decorative accent to the outdoor room.

ARCHITECTURAL elements

When real estate agents want

to woo prospective buyers to a property, they advertise its most desirable features first. Thus the phrase "wood-burning fireplace" invariably leads the ad copy. And because fireplaces are such highly sought amenities, builders have wised up and included a "WBFP" in even the most economical homes. So finding a home with an indoor fireplace isn't too difficult. But finding a home that offers a wood-burning fireplace outside is a discovery.

An outdoor fireplace, perhaps more

than any other feature, transforms an exterior space into an outdoor room. Immediately the location—whether a patio or deck adjoined to the house, a pavilion out in the lawn, or simply a new fireplace wall anywhere on the grounds—gains a focal point and becomes a gathering place. The sensory appeals of the fire are hard to resist: the smell of wood smoke, the warmth of the embers, the mesmerizing flicker of the red flame. The fireplace often inspires the creation of a great-room—an open area with both living and dining functions (and sometimes a kitchen). Which area is closest to the fireplace is a matter of homeowner discretion. The important factor is that both spaces have a view of the fire.

Because most older homes

do not include outdoor fireplaces among their selling points, acquiring this feature usually means adding it on. The options, thankfully, are many. Everything from an architect-designed chimney wall to match the house to a freestanding fireplace purchased at a home improvement store is available. In between those two in scope and budget lie do-it-yourself fireplaces built from project books. Whichever type of fireplace suits your practicability, there is this guarantee: The fireplace is certain to transform your outdoors into an outdoor room.

HEARTH = home

1) PUEBLO ARCHITECTURE'S kiva fireplaces inspired this grand yet simple design. Instead of building only a fireplace, the homeowners constructed an adobe wall that extends many feet to either side of the relatively small arched firebox. A hearth spans the entire wall, which towers up to match the height of the home itself. The structure even includes sconce lighting and a small window. Despite the massive scale, an absence of embellishment on the adobe wall still conveys a simplicity inherent to Pueblo design.

2) ANOTHER SOUTHWESTERN-STYLE home takes a scaled-down approach to its outdoor fireplace. A small arched firebox is cut into an exterior wall that's part of the house. To take up the least amount of space, the fireplace is raised to eye level and doesn't include a hearth.

THIS FIREPLACE illustrates how easily a structure can be added without impinging upon the existing architecture. Located on the property line, the fireplace is freestanding. It is positioned much like a gate, as a natural break in the fencing, which picks up on either side. The fireplace's style is clean and classic, like the design of the house it serves. Its presence provides an orientation for the outdoor living space, with the main conversation area directly in front of it.

INSIDE OUT DECORATING OUTDOOR SPACES WITH INDOOR STYLE

1) LIKE A FAIRY-TALE TOWER, this river-rock fireplace rises up to greet the day. The natural stones blend into the environment, just as the tower's shape echoes the peaks of the surrounding hillsides. Key to the structure's success is its location on the edge of the property, along the rock garden wall. This location defines the back boundary of the outdoor room created by the fireplace.

2) THE FIREPLACE is a stylistic extension of the house, which features an abundance of the same natural stone. When a house makes a strong style statement like this one, elements of the outdoor rooms will blend best when built with the same materials.

1) THERE IS MORE LATITUDE for the size and shape of an outdoor fireplace than is possible for an indoor fireplace. A case in point, outdoors a fire ring is an option to a more conventional firebox.

2) NOT EVERYONE has the space or budget to build a fireplace into their outdoor architecture. An increasing number of portable fireplaces means outdoor fires can be enjoyed just the same. Freestanding fireplaces, such as this gel-fueled copper model, are available in a wide range of styles and materials, at affordable price points.

An outdoor room, by definition, is a living space outside the home with at least one side left open; often all four sides are open. The roof may be left open, partially covered, or defined by another airier overhead structure such as a pergola. Even when the outdoor room is open on all sides and above, completely exposed to the fresh air, it still must have boundaries to distinguish it from its surroundings.

These boundaries can be created using such elements as architectural salvage. Old stained-glass windows or chipped-paint columns not only serve as decorative accents, but they denote a perimeter and suggest a wall without the closed-in look and feel. Folksy birdhouses on posts do the same trick. Fabric panels, canopies, and tents are other alternatives that clearly carve outdoor spaces into rooms. More subtle, green plants can grace the landscape to break up the outdoors into intimate rooms. These green walls are as effective as real walls in defining the boundaries of an outdoor room, but with none of architecture's man-made intrusion.

Finally the most clearly asserted outdoor boundaries come in the form of a gazebo's walls and roof. Other structures, such as pergolas, pavilions, arbors, and porches, also are rooms grafted onto the landscape. Their partial or transparent walls, railings, and ceilings are slightly less confining (but no less definitive) than gazebos. Along with gazebos, many can be purchased from kits sold at home improvement, garden, or mass merchandise stores.

This section introduces examples of the above solutions for creating walls, or the idea of walls, to define outdoor rooms. See which ones work best for you.

If you would be happy all your life—plant a garden.

1) THIS PERGOLA OFFERS no protection from the elements, but its architecture leaves the impression of a full-fledged room. The colonnade, lattice sides, stick ceiling over shaped beams, and raised platform floor work together to produce an entity with a distinct character, in this case, one of classical beauty and quiet charm. Twig chairs softened with cushions and huddled together in a conversation circle make the pergola an ideal retreat for catch-up sessions with friends or family.

2) ANY WAY YOU LOOK, this gazebo provides picture-postcard vistas of vacation fun. Commanding views of the swimming pool and ocean, the structure offers an easy walk to either one. Mosquito netting tied back as curtain panels looks decorative but becomes significantly functional when enlisted into use. A blue and white striped outdoor area rug brightens the floor and is impervious to water damage at the same time. When it's dirty, simply hose it down.

ARCHITECTURE IN A KIT

Does this sound familiar: You love the look of a custom gazebo, but don't have the budget for an architect and a builder? You'll be pleased to know there's now an alternative. An architect-designed gazebo is now available at a fraction of the cost.

Renowned architect Michael Graves has put his name behind several outdoor rooms. They're not cheap (at least $6,000 for the materials), but they're far less than a custom Graves design. And to prove there's a move towards all-America accessibility in the home-design field, the pavilions are available through Lindal Cedar Homes, a major home manufacturer. To see the pavilions, go to *lindal.com/graves*

1) ALL GAZEBOS ARE not created equal, at least in terms of style. This charmer has a rustic quality that harkens back to fairy tales or, more recently, to the great camps in the Adirondacks prevalent in Upstate New York at the end of the 19th century. The entire structure, including its furnishings, is built from logs and twigs with the bark still attached. Keeping things simple, the furniture consists entirely of built-in benches, except for a single small table. It's a place for quietly appreciating nature with as little indoor baggage to distract as possible.

2) THIS VIEW HAS TO TOP anyone's list of favorites. The gazebo overlooks the ocean, with flowering plants and scented firs snuggling up close. Gingerbread trim and crisp white paint make it the quintessential gazebo.

1) **THE GLORY** of the garden is the theme of this gazebo. Plunked square in the midst of a yard full of lush plantings, it's a prime observation point for all that grows in every direction in this lovingly tended garden.

2) **EVEN THOUGH** it's close to the house, the gazebo doesn't repeat the home's paint palette or architectural style. A little more fanciful, it's an escape from, rather than an extension of, the house. The subdued color scheme defines but doesn't overstate the case for difference.

1) HANGING STAINED-GLASS WINDOWS and architectural salvage increase the definition of this pergola as an outdoor room. Both help to hem in the open area, acting as walls without being opaque. Rose bushes growing up a low stacked-rock wall reinforce one of the pergola's boundaries with sweet-scented pastel beauty.

2) AN OLD STAINED-GLASS panel sparkles as the sunlight passes through, intensifying the visual pleasures inside the pergola. Its shape spans the narrow vertical opening at one end of the pergola just enough to suggest enclosure, but not so much as to block the enticing view.

INSIDE OUT DECORATING OUTDOOR SPACES WITH INDOOR STYLE

3

**3) STAINED-GLASS AND
LATTICE PANELS** stand in for solid
walls on this open-air porch, creating a
stronger sense of separation without
blocking the views.

1) A POOLSIDE PAVILION offers shelter from the rain as well as a superb perch for watching sunsets, nature, and children in the pool. Its red-tile roof ties in with the Mediterranean architecture of the house and also creates a stately villa presence for the structure. Unlike gazebos, pavilions are completely open on the sides. Even the four structural supports—shown here as substantial white columns—contribute to the formal Mediterranean design.

2) JUST BEYOND THE BACK DOOR, a tile-roofed Mediterranean-style dining pavilion, complete with chandelier, continues the design and living function of the home outdoors, where the views are unsurpassable.

3) PAVILIONS AREN'T JUST FOR POOLS. This dining pavilion is nearly flush with the house, so stepping out for a meal requires minimal effort. Though new, it features a Victorian design that complements the house's Victorian architecture. Homeowners can add a similar pavilion anywhere there is an existing patio: Only four posts and an enclosed or partially enclosed roof are essential.

4) THE PAVILION also goes the extra mile with decoration. It utilizes turned posts, finials, gingerbread, molding, and a cut-out panel to re-create a Victorian look. Multiple paint colors complete the period effect.

1) WHEN THE PRIVACY of a wall is sometimes, but not always, desired for an outdoor room, fabric can provide a best-of-both-worlds answer. Unfurl the weatherproof awning-stripe panel and tie it to a porch post when it's time to be sheltered from the bright sun, a breeze, or neighbors' eyes. When it's time to open up, the fabric rolls up like a window shade, returning the room to its open-air status.

2) NOT QUITE A GREENHOUSE but rather an outdoor garden room, this whimsical structure is nothing more than mosquito netting fitted to a skeletal frame. High finials at either end and pagoda-style ornamentation at the entry create an attractive Asian ambience.

3) TENTS PROVIDE the most doable of all outdoor rooms. This one, more canopy than tent, is familiar to campers who've long known the advantage of setting up an open-air pavilion in addition to their closed-in sleeping tents. Mounted like a tent with poles, stakes, and ties, the canopy is equally appropriate at home or on the campground. This white canopy, decked as a dining hall, creates a celebratory feel in any backyard.

1

1) THE LANDSCAPE PLAYS as much of a role in identifying the boundaries of this outdoor dining room as does the pergola that shelters it. Certainly the pergola starts the definition of the space. The bike on the long wall and the greenery growing alongside and over the pergola further its uniqueness from the surroundings. The greenery atop the pergola beams also integrates the outdoor room into the environment. So there exists a design irony: The same greenery that distinguishes the pergola as a separate entity also weaves it into its setting.

2) A TANGLE OF VINES and other climbing plants blankets the support posts and eaves of this multipurpose outdoor pavilion by the pool. Even though the architecture defines the room, the greenery furthers its distinction. Its lush plant life and strong color contrast with the adjoining pale brick house.

2

INSIDE OUT DECORATING OUTDOOR SPACES WITH INDOOR STYLE

3) IN BOTH of these settings, plant life denotes the perimeters of the outdoor rooms. Trees, shrubs, and flowering foliage all get into the act. They hem in two intimate spaces providing views of well-engineered, lavish landscaping.

3

ORGANIC ARCHITECTURE

If you're a naturalist and want as few man-made structures as possible imposing on your landscape, consider using plant life as a substitute for architecture to create an outdoor room.

For the most privacy, design a landscape plan that surrounds all sides of the proposed outdoor room, leaving just enough space for an entry.

The simplest plan is one with a square or rectangular shape, only as big as you want the room "inside." For a different look, consider other shapes that are not feasible with hard walls. Kidney-shaped rooms, teardrops, diamonds, ovals, and circles require more effort but can be dramatic. Before choosing an alternative shape, however, realistically appraise your gardening skills and your willingness to spend time on maintenance. For the more complex geometric shapes to retain a crisp definition, the plant life must thrive. The shapes must be accurately identified and the greenery planted at precise places for the definition to read clearly. Consider these points:

•For a formal look, define your room with boxwood. A square- or rectangular-shaped space works best for this plant.

•Use a row of trees along one side of the outdoor room for a dramatic backdrop.

•Encircle a small room with flowers, and for vertical definition add baskets of plants on decorative posts.

•For simplicity, outline the boundaries with one medium-height shrub, such as a variety of yew.

•For more complexity, plant boundaries with varying texture, color, and height of the plant materials. (Plant the lowest plants on the inside, facing the room—the opposite of a fenceline border.)

2

1) THIS ZEN-STYLE PAVILION
proves a point: An outdoor room can, and ideally should, fit an individual's design style and lifestyle. Instead of a generic square box, an Asian ambience was chosen. The look was easy to achieve. To a basic, bare-bones pavilion, all that was added were wood-grid partitions, akin to French doors but stationary. And instead of clear glass panes inside each grid, milky, translucent nonglare acrylic panels evoke the look of rice paper screens.

2) THE FURNISHINGS ARE AS SIMPLE as the pavilion's architecture. A clean-lined wood chair and coffee table, in the same natural wood hue as the pavilion, honor the integrity of their design and materials.

Tip: Use your patio's or garden's paving material to erect the "walls" of your outdoor room. Stack the same stone or bricks used as flooring into small walls just taller than a curb, in the desired shape of the room you want.

1) HIGH WALLS with 90-degree angles aren't the only kind that can create an outdoor room. A low, spiraling rock wall forms the small sitting room. It circumscribes the room and also creates much of the aesthetic appeal of the larger backyard. The final coil of the wall, where it turns in itself, is a relatively small feature yet it's the wall's strongest design statement.

2) THE STACKED-STONE WALL is on the same axis as the path leading to the home's back door—a fact that aids the wall in creating a courtyard effect. Looking through the home's French doors, one sees brick-paved paths terminating in the circular, stone-bordered sitting room, with the extra-tall privacy fence just behind suggesting a courtyard more than a small backyard.

THE OUTDOOR DINING AREA at this home is only a small corner of the patio. How is the feel of a separate room created without a wall to divide the dining space from the rest of the patio? Two ways. First the table is tucked in close to one exterior wall of the house, toward the corner. This orientation frees up the remainder of the patio for other use. Second the old louvered doors pulled up to the wall act as a decorative screen, further defining the dining space. The silvery hue of the architectural salvage matches the finish of the table and chairs, pulling the elements together to establish a strong visual element.

Tip: Create a sense of separateness for an outdoor room by positioning the furniture close to a corner of the house. Then underscore the area as apart with architectural salvage. Put old columns, stained-glass windows, or doors between the wall of the house and the outdoor room to function as a screen and to give the area an extra dimension of definition.

Just as walls, or the insinuation of walls, help define an outdoor room, so does the ground underfoot. Unlike walls or their close kin, which only skim the perimeters of a room, flooring literally covers every inch of the space. That's why it's important to give this architectural feature equal attention when designing your outdoor room.

Options for outdoor flooring actually are broader than those for indoor rooms. Natural stones and woods, painted flooring, area rugs, wall-to-wall carpets, and ceramic tiles—all the standards for indoors—are available in waterproof outdoor varieties. Sisal-look synthetic carpets can cover an entire outdoor space. The newest crop of striped, solid, or whimsical-print area rugs also are waterproof. But in addition, materials typically not used inside, such as brick pavers, pea gravel, poured concrete, stone-and-grass combinations, or widely creative tile and stone mosaics too bumpy for use indoors, deepen the pool of available flooring materials for outdoors.

In deciding on a material, consider the style of the house and the rest of the landscape. Then pick a flooring material that's compatible. That doesn't mean the flooring has to be inconspicuous. A dramatic contrast may be your goal. At the other extreme, you may want a material that defines the outdoor room without detracting the eye from the overall environment—one that's low-key. You may want the flooring to be entirely different for the outdoor room than for any other outdoor space, to really call attention to its separateness. Or you may want it to be a continuation of the material used elsewhere in the landscape and garden —sort of like wall-to-wall carpeting installed throughout an entire home for a seamless look.

1) A FAUX-PAINTED AREA RUG brings sparkling style to this outdoor living room. The imaginative floor treatment begins with ordinary decking, stained gray. Just like a textile rug, the decking serves as the neutral ground for the painted rug's motifs. In the middle of the decking, a painted medallion with a cameo-style portrait in its center creates the focal point for both the rug and room. A pattern painted along the edges of the decking delineates the border of the faux rug. Note: The room's flooring ends where the room does; the step leading to the next outdoor room is signaled by a change in flooring materials from wood decking to slate tiles.

2) POURED CONCRETE PATIO FLOORING becomes a canvas for creativity in this beautifully decorated outdoor living room. Painted with a trompe l'oeil stone-floor design, the boring concrete is elevated to a new level of fun. Now the floor is as much of a decorative asset to the room as the lattice panels and art on the walls.

1) **THE UNUSUAL QUALITY** of the outdoor living room that's articulated on the floor is repeated in the furnishings. This salvaged window becomes a one-of-a-kind tabletop.

2) **TO CREATE** a three-dimensional floor in this outdoor living room, a combination of stone and grass is used. Irregular cut stones are laid far enough apart to permit a sizable border of grass to grow in the crevices. The grass continues the greenery of the lawn beyond the room for a smooth transition, and the stones establish the room as a discrete space. The only drawback? A little mowing is required as maintenance.

3) INDIVIDUAL OUTDOOR LIVING areas such as this are scattered throughout the property. Repetition of the grass-and-stone paving in each space ensures visual continuity. Walls of hedges and art or architectural elements, such as the pair of tall iron espaliers flanking the stone bench, declare the boundaries of each room.

1) THE SAME COMBINATION of grass-edged stone shown on page 159 is put to a different purpose at this picturesque country house: It is used as wall-to-wall carpeting, connecting all areas of the landscape as well as flooring each of the property's outdoor rooms. The long stone pathway shown here winds around the hedgerow maze to a sitting area furnished with a pair of Adirondack chairs—an outdoor room floored in the same combination of grass-edged stone.

2) TO AVOID ANY BREAK in the beauty of the landscape, the same flooring connects the front and back sides of the property. When the wooden gate dividing the front from the back is open, the eye travels without disruption from one space to the next.

GETTING grounded

1) WHEN AN OUTDOOR ROOM
is located some distance away from the
house instead of just outside the door
on a patio or deck, paths must help
define traffic flow to and from the room.
This attractive approach is created
using concrete-stone aggregate tiles as
the stepping stones, with decorative red
rock as filler on the sides. Laying the
tiles on the diagonal creates a more
interesting look.

2

3

2) WEATHERED WOOD DECKING continues from the main deck as pathways connecting to the outdoor rooms in the garden.

3) ANOTHER OPTION for a traffic lane leading up to an outdoor room is tile (or stone) laid a stride's length apart. The tiles shown here are decoratively painted with a white diamond motif on a blue background—a scheme in harmony with the blue and white palette of the gazebo flooring (a step is just visible on the left).

1) RED BRICK PAVERS are a classic, hardy flooring material for outdoor rooms, as this pavilion illustrates. To make the flooring more dramatic, experiment with patterns, laying the pavers in different configurations before setting them.

2) THE SAME PAVILION would acquire an entirely different look if covered wall-to-wall in an outdoor carpet like any of these. All are synthetic, waterproof, and mold-resistant. When they become soiled, simply spray off dirt with a hose.

1) ON A COVERED PORCH, an indoor area rug (provided it's not too fragile) can create a cozy conversation area. Choose rugs with patterns that forgive dirt, and choose fibers and weaves that are sturdy enough to withstand heavy wear.

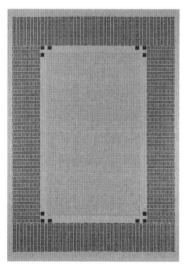

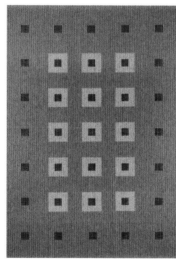

2) FOR OUTDOOR ROOMS that are not covered, area rugs crafted from synthetic mildew-resistant fibers can create the same coziness as indoor area rugs. Maintenance is easy: Simply hose off the rugs when they begin to show dirt or mud.

DECORATIVE elements

Function:

Fabric is an essential building block in turning an outdoor area into a room. In the simplest design, it is used to upholster cushions and pillows, imparting both visual and physical softness to furniture that is typically hard and neutral. In more complex designs, it is used to canopy a space or furnishing, sometimes puddling to the floor like a lavish indoor window dressing. One of fabric's important functions is to inject color and/or pattern to the outdoor space. Often, it is the only option to fill that role, in the absence of indoor decorative elements such as wallpaper or painted wall finishes. Through repetition, fabric can be a transitional device that weaves together different parts of an outdoor room. In addition to these decorative functions, fabric also can serve a utilitarian role, protecting from bugs and sun, and adding privacy where desired.

Fiber:

Unlike indoor fabrics, those used in outdoor rooms have to withstand rain and direct sunlight unless stored during inclement weather or protected by a shelter. The weatherproof fabrics are synthetic and rated according to performance. The most hard-working fabrics are found on umbrellas and as upholstery on furniture that's stationary during the season (not pulled into storage in bad weather). More liberty can be taken with decorative pillows, which can be easily stashed in a storm. They can be covered with natural fibers for maximum softness and variety in appearance, and trimmed with dressmaker details, including gimping, buttons, pleats, and ruffles.

1) BECAUSE OF THEIR VERSATILITY, stripes remain the most popular outdoor fabric for cushions and sling chairs or loungers. Classic yet informal, they work equally well with traditional, contemporary, and country styles.

2) FOREST GREEN, white, or two-tone awning stripes no longer are the only options in weatherproof umbrella fabrics. Pinstripes, florals, and jewel tones join the mix, which manufacturers are constantly expanding.

3) **MORE MUTED PALETTES,** coupled with active patterns, are now readily available alternatives among weatherproof fabrics.

4) **CLOTH DINNER NAPKINS** are an easy way to introduce, change, or mix colors and patterns for outdoor dining occasions.

WITHSTANDING THE WEATHER

When it comes to fabric, outdoors is not the place to be organic. That's because organic material serves as a food source for mold; when moisture is added, and the temperature is right (all year in many regions), mold will grow. So instead of natural fibers such as cotton, linen, and wool, which will mildew after a rain, synthetics are the best bet for durability outdoors.

•**ACRYLIC:** This is the top-of-the-line fabric for outdoors. In its most sophisticated forms, flatweave and linear acrylic can withstand 1,000 sunlight hours and not fade. Acrylic is mildew-resistant. Brand-name fabrics are coated with a moisture- and stain-resistant finish.

•**SPUN POLYESTER:** A close second to acrylic, spun polyester can last 500 hours in the sun. Unlike acrylic, polyester-vinyl fabrics don't require a protective coating to repel moisture and resist mold and mildew.

Even though synthetics are mildew-resistant, in areas of heavy rainfall it's still a good idea to bring cushions indoors or to a protected space to lengthen their life span. Even though the upholstery fabric may repel moisture, the padding in cushions may be less successful.

1) **PLAYING DRESS-UP** means piling on the feminine fabrics. For special occasions, organic fabrics like cotton shears with flocked-velvet polka dots make stunning table skirts. Here an everyday painted-iron table is transformed into a furnishing fit for the most romantic bridal shower or delightful afternoon tea. Old garden chairs are freshened in minutes with swaths of cloth draped across their backs then tied on with ribbons, each one accented with two fresh roses. A coordinated underskirt for the table and matching floral napkins are the final touches that prove fabric's power in fashioning romance.

2 & 3) **THIS MAKEOVER** from an everyday outdoor table to a romantic table for two requires nothing but a floral tablecloth and two expanses of sheers (sheer window panels will do). The sheers are wrapped over the sides and backs of the iron chairs as instant no-sew slipcovers. Allowing them to cascade onto the lawn enhances the romantic effect.

2) **OUTDOOR ROOMS** are as entitled to privacy as their indoor counterparts. This porch on one side faces neighbors. So when more privacy is desired, a cotton-sheet panel pulls closed, blocking the view and also shielding the porch from the sun.

3) **HERE FABRIC SERVES** as architecture covering the pergola with eye-catching swags that shade the area from the sun. The visual rhythm of the undulating fabric softens the hard edges of the space, adding drama through curves. It also provides the room's only source of color and pattern.

1) **BEGINNING WITH** the sunny striped canopy, fabric is the essence of this outdoor dining room. The canopy defines the perimeters of the space and shelters it from the sun. The vibrant striped fabric repeats as tied-back panels framing the doorways of a nearby porch give the entire patio area visual continuity.

To keep the look clean and simple but continuous, the fabric appears a third time on the chair cushions. Big bows with long streamers tie the cushions onto the backs of the iron chairs with classic charm.

4) **TALL TWIG POLES** topped with a weatherproof striped fabric canopy create an outdoor room easily and efficiently. Adding fabric also adds color and movement to the space.

No outdoor room is complete without furniture, but furniture alone doesn't make an outdoor space a room. To be transforming, the furniture must enhance the area's aesthetics and increase its comfort. With softening cushions, a pleasing palette, and a conversational arrangement that addresses lifestyle needs, the furniture takes the space to the next step in creating the sense of a room. Thanks to responsive manufacturers, the options among outdoor furnishings are as great as ever.

The widest selection of furniture is for sheltered spaces such as gazebos, porches, or loggias, which have the protection of a roof. Furniture used here need not be weather-resistant, however; at the same time, it should not be fine. Wicker, twig, and rattan—all earthy materials—are naturals here. Painted furniture, too susceptible to the elements to go unsheltered, also works in protected outdoor arenas.

Among weatherproof furnishings, today's offerings accommodate diversity in personal style. Convincing synthetic wicker makes a cottage statement; cast iron and teak support traditional designs; aluminum speaks to contemporary tastes; and stained or painted wood and resin furnishings establish a more generic garden look. Teak goes beyond a pretty bench in an English garden and is now being fashioned in contemporary styles for the patio and deck. Classics like the Adirondack chair and the canvas sling hold ground while joined by such newcomers as the ergonomically correct mesh lounger that's a spin-off of a popular office chair design. Mixed-medium furnishings that combine aluminum framing with a weatherproof wood-like teak are becoming popular, offering both comfort and style.

1) AN AMERICAN CLASSIC, the Adirondack chair originated in the 19th century at the summer homes (known as "great camps") in the Adirondack Mountains of Upstate New York. It has been a strong favorite since, and its popularity is spreading across the country. Essentially a hard slat-back, slat-seat chair, it can be placed in a circular arrangement and seats and backs softened with pillows. A grouping of the chairs leaves no doubt that the outdoor space is a living room. Painted white, the chairs work well with cottage architecture. Because of the simplicity of their design, they also can be used with traditional, country, and even contemporary architecture.

2

3

2) VINTAGE METAL CHAIRS carve out a room on a deck thanks to two factors: the fire-engine red color and their circular arrangement. The tree-stump-turned-table serves as a focal point of the gathering and proves furnishing outdoors can be just as creative as any indoor endeavor.

3) ANTIQUES CAN BE just as compatible with the outdoors as they are with interiors. An antique French garden chair and a chipped-paint table only improve in appearance with weathering. For a home filled with antiques, they provide a continuum from inside to out.

TAKE CARE

•**ALUMINUM:** Prolong the life of the protective coating on aluminum outdoor furniture by keeping it clean and treating it with car wax. Never use ammonia or window cleaners, which contain ammonia.

Touch up scratches with exterior metal paint. "Powder" finishes, however, require touch-up paint from the manufacturer.

•**CAST IRON AND STEEL:** These will rust, so inspect them often, especially around welded joints. If you find rust, sand the area, prime, and coat with a rust-resistant metal paint rated for outdoor use. Then treat with a car or spray wax.

•**WICKER:** Remove dust from both natural and synthetic wicker with a vacuum or soft-bristled brush. Or scrub with soap and water. Organic wicker cracks when dry. Treat dryness with boiled linseed oil, then wipe dry.

•**TEAK:** Do nothing. Allow to gray with age. Do not oil, as this encourages mildew.

•**PAINTED OR STAINED WOOD:** Clean with soap and water.

•**RESIN:** Apply car wax to prevent stains from permeating the porous plastic. Scrub stains with a mild detergent.

•**CUSHIONS:** Acrylic cushion covers such as Sunbrella are coated with a moisture- and stain-resistant finish that detergents remove, so clean with a gentle soap. If mildewed, wash with ½ cup nonchlorine bleach in 5 gallons of water; then reapply an outdoor-fabric finish. Polyester-vinyl fabrics, such as Textilene, don't need this coating; clean with soapy water.

FURNITURE

1) SYNTHETIC WICKER offers the look of the natural material but with weather resistance. This porch grouping can stay outside all year long, without a moisture problem. The upholstery fabric is a solution-dyed acrylic that wicks off moisture yet feels soft like cotton.

2) AVAILABLE IN A RANGE of colors, including forest green, synthetic wicker contrasts nicely with wood furnishings to create comfortable, relaxing outdoor settings.

3) FOR SHELTERED AREAS, natural white-painted wicker offers a classic look.

Tip: Seed an old wooden coffee or side table with grass to keep your green thumb in shape. Choose an open location where your grass-topped table can soak up the sun and rain.

1) ONE-OF-A-KIND FURNITURE can be created readily from found materials, such as this flat chunk of limestone. Used as a tabletop, the mossy limestone is impervious to moisture and wear and tear.

2) ANOTHER UNIQUE TABLETOP idea is a mosaic created from broken pots and china. Laid over an inexpensive wood table, the shards weatherproof the surface while forming a work of art.

2) IRON AND RESIN are combined on this outdoor table and chairs. The contrast in materials and colors makes the grouping stand out in its wooded setting.

2

1

1) ALUMINUM FRAMES with vinyl webbing are a cool outdoor furniture option at an affordable price. The look, too, is airy and light.

4) **FOLDING LAWN FURNITURE** has the ability to create an outdoor room on a blanket of green grass. This furniture offers decorative interest with its pattern and color. Its fabric slings also soften the space.

3) **OUTDOOR FURNITURE** can take an architectural turn, as this built-in tile-clad banquette shows. The strong lines and flowing color give the piece the look of a frozen waterfall.

1) SLEEK-LINED LOUNGERS made from teak are at home in this contemporary outdoor poolside room. The furniture's broad proportions offer maximum comfort, and the hand-waxed finish speaks of quiet luxury.

2) GENEROUS SEATING proportions and oversize cushions on this settee and high-back chairs mean the same comfort enjoyed indoors now can be savored outside. The look is elegant, with the simple but curvaceous mahogany designs that have been coated in a clear wood preservative.

The furniture grouping, without aid of any other decorative or architectural elements, transforms a patio into a full-fledged outdoor room.

3) ORIGINALLY USED on office furniture, woven fabric on an aluminum frame has been engineered for UV stability, outdoor use, and a comfortable, breathable texture. It offers support to the body, encouraging blissful relaxation.

To be a well-dressed room,

an outdoor living space requires art and accessories as finishing touches. These decorative details, however small, go a long way in imbuing an outdoor room with distinct personality, distinguishing it from a generic patio or deck.

Walls can be used for displaying art

outdoors, especially walls under the eaves of the house. They make semi-protected backdrops for weather-resistant art including multimedia panels utilizing such materials as clay, wire, and redwood. Or display more expected artwork like terra-cotta wall-mounted sculptures and fountains. The walls of loggias and porches expand the options further to include artwork that's less weather-resistant.

What if an outdoor room has no walls? Use sculpture

to help define the space as well as increase its character as a real room.

Similarly, accessories can be sprinkled wherever

appropriate. Birdhouses, seashells and rocks, potted plants, and colorful watering cans are just some of the possibilities suited for outdoor decorating.

ART & ACCESSORIES

INSIDE OUT DECORATING OUTDOOR SPACES WITH INDOOR STYLE

1

1) **DECORATING** the back wall of this lattice-work pavilion with a mirror, sconces, an antique china platter, and a print announces a room setting as decoratively pleasing as any found indoors. More accessories line the pair of shelves on one of the pavilion's open sides, framing the room with decorative details that entertain the eye. Tabletops are enlisted, too, for books, pottery, and more plants to create an ambience akin to an indoor living room or sunroom.

2) **ON THE OPPOSITE END** of the pavilion, straw hats on what is literally a hat tree or twig add aesthetic accents, along with baskets, pottery, and other collectibles.

3) **ART AND OBJETS D'ART** displayed on the back wall of a courtyard define that portion of the courtyard as an outdoor sitting area.

4) **EVEN THE WALL** of a house can serve as a backdrop for art displays, transforming a bland patio into a discrete outdoor living space.

2

3

1) CLEVERLY DISPLAYED gardening paraphernalia dresses up a porch as appealingly as fine art or more typical indoor accessories. A piece of architectural salvage propped on the tabletop to meet the hanging watering cans and wash tub, and dramatizes the whole display.

2) ORNAMENTAL GRASS planted in a time-worn sugar mold makes a beautifully simple statement as the centerpiece on an outdoor dining room's table.

3) POTTED IN AN OLD PAIL that has an interesting rusted patina, a rose bush provides a finishing touch to an outdoor living room.

1, 2 & 3) A CENTURIES-OLD idea, such as an elaborately carved stone garden fountain, finds new life as one of the decorative extras that turns an outdoor space into a real room. While the intricate stonework is appealing, consider buying a functioning fountain or reconditioning an old one. The sound of gently splashing water disguises street noises to make time spent in your outdoor room even more pleasant and relaxing.

1

2

4

③

⑤ ⑥

4, 5 & 6) ARCHITECTURAL NICHES and ledges serve as platforms for sculpture or pottery, enhancing the finished feel of an outdoor room. Cluster objects to create interesting vignettes, and rearrange the groupings from time to time to keep the view fresh.

In interior decorating, lighting too

often is an overlooked element when, in fact, it should be an integral part of any space's design. Not only does the same principle apply to outdoor decorating, but it does so in spades. Lighting, as shown in "Good by Night" (pages 84–91), is a decorating element with an essential function for outdoor designs: It is the single element that makes an outdoor room as livable by night as it is by day.

Plus, the right kind of lighting goes a long way in contribut-

ing to the outdoor room's aesthetics, setting the mood. A crystal chandelier instantly brings elegance to the outdoor room; a strand of sparkling stars or chili-pepper lights defines the outdoor room as a place for casual celebrations; a wrought-iron candelier can lend a romantic or country ambience, depending upon the rest of the decor.

The choices for outdoor lighting include electric

chandeliers and sconces, "candeliers" (chandeliers with candles instead of lightbulbs), electric floor and table lamps, lanterns, torches, hurricane lamps, candles, battery-charged canister lights, strands of tiny white lights, or more whimsical motifs such as fish or chili peppers, and spots.

Electric chandeliers and sconces

require access to an outlet, so these may not work in every outdoor situation. Whenever they can be used, however, they imbue the space with the feel of indoors. Chandeliers and candeliers both require some overhead structure, such as a pergola or loggia, for mounting, although a little creativity can overcome that obstacle—even a sturdy branch can be enlisted to support the fixture. Outdoor electric floor and table lamps are grounded to eliminate shocking and are weighted to withstand winds, so they are safe bets anywhere outdoors within reach of an outlet (or within the reach of an outlet by a long extension cord).

Strands of lights provide a beautiful way to define the perimeter of an outdoor room. Use them along rooftops, down beams, across deck railings, and around umbrellas. Battery-charged canister lights look good lining a deck rail, or as tabletop lighting. Battery- or solar-powered ground lights work not only to light an approach to an outdoor space, but to outline the outdoor room itself.

Candles provide the most romantic light, but in a breeze, they are best used in the protection of a hurricane lamp. Lanterns and torches are fun when entertaining, and citronella-scented varieties also ward off mosquitoes.

So which lighting solution is best

for your outdoor room? Experiment. A combination of different lights will provide the most drama, function, and fun.

1) ELEGANCE IS introduced into this outdoor dining room with the simple addition of a single, striking crystal chandelier. The unexpectedness of the gorgeous fixture, where more rugged lighting typically reigns, only increases its charm.

4) **THERE'S NO NEED** to settle for an outdoor chandelier that doesn't precisely articulate your outdoor room's decorating style. A hybrid, this chandelier lantern teams the traditional chandelier design with the rusticity of a lantern—an apt combination to promote the room's classical Mediterranean design.

2 & 3) **A WROUGHT-IRON CHANDELIER** gives this portable, easy-does-it outdoor dining room all the dignity and drama of a more permanent structure. It completes the space's transformation from simply an outdoor area to an outdoor room. It also sets a mood. With all its candles burning, the fixture casts the cottage-country table and chairs beneath it in an unmistakably romantic light.

1) **BATTERY-CHARGED** canister lights, sprinkled directly onto the ground, illuminate an outdoor hot tub room. The lights have the advantage of no unsightly wiring or need for proximity to an electrical outlet. They do, however, require frequent recharging, making them a higher-maintenance choice.

2) **A PAIR OF** matching faux-bamboo lamps—one a floor model and the other a table style—flanks this outdoor living room's settee rocker. Both lamps are weighted to keep them in place and are grounded for safety to make them shock-resistant even in rain. Both the shades and bases are water-repellent, allowing the lamps to be left outdoors even in a downpour. The bamboo motif reflects outdoor products' increasing ability to stay current with indoor decorating trends.

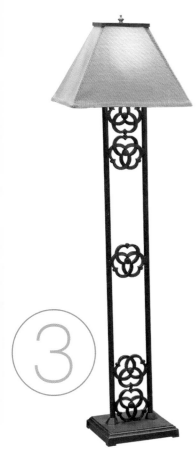

3) **BUILT FOR OUTDOORS,** this classic iron floor lamp is versatile enough to work with a variety of decorating styles, including many traditional, Arts and Crafts, country, and even contemporary designs.

4) **A ROPE-STYLE** table lamp anchors an outdoor space with real-room style. Its casual look suggests a country style with a nautical theme.

1) VINYL LANTERNS have the look of Japanese rice paper but are durable enough for outdoor wear. The citrus palette shown here adds a refreshing shot of color to complete the outdoor design.

2) INSTEAD OF simply emulating interior design, outdoor decorating sometimes seems strongest when it celebrates its unique roots in nature. One way of doing that is to take liberties that might be deemed kitsch or over-the-top indoors but, outdoors, are just great fun. Strands of small lantern lights festooned on an umbrella table spell that kind of celebration.

2

1

Tip: Enlist unexpected household items as candleholders. Look through your kitchen catch-all drawer or a cache of odds-and-ends pottery for ideas.

1) REPURPOSED OBJECTS make intriguing candleholders, causing the eye to look twice. Objects that cluster candles, candelabra-style, increase visibility accordingly.

2) TEA LIGHTS floating with pansy petals in shallow terra-cotta pots bring nature's best colors to this creative lighting solution.

3) POWERED BY rechargeable batteries, these outdoor light canisters eliminate the need for other light sources (especially harsher overhead lighting or floodlights). Though they offer a similar subtle lighting, the canisters are more hassle-free than candles, which are subject to blowing out in the wind or rain.

When an outdoor room meant

nothing more than a couple of chairs plopped out on the deck or patio, picking a palette wasn't overly important. Since nothing about the outdoor area resembled indoor design anyway, continuity wasn't an issue. A few standards, such as green and white awning stripes, sufficed from one decade to the next. That's no longer true.

Green and white stripes are

still an outdoor staple, to be sure. Now, however, when outdoor rooms are designed as indoor rooms, continuity matters. That simplifies the process of picking a palette: For outdoor rooms visible from the inside of the house, the palette may be an exact repetition or simplification of the indoor colors.

That's an easy approach,

but not the only one. A neutral palette may be desired outdoors to better blend with the landscape, even though the house is colorful inside. Take, for example, cottage design. The interior is a rainbow of pastels, while the exterior is crisp, white clapboard. The outdoor living room can either repeat the interior pastels or echo the clean white of the home's facade.

On larger lots where an outdoor room is not

located within clear view of the house, take more liberty with the palette as there's no danger of jarring juxtapositions of colors. In a poolside cabana, use colors that brighten anything in the house. Or in a vine-covered dining pergola, make the palette softer and more romantic than the hues inside. If a room is in full sun, colors will fade on all but the most resilient outdoor fabrics, so pick a shade brighter than what you might normally choose.

Tip: Consider every element in the landscape—especially flower color in the garden—when deciding on a palette for an outdoor room. Choose a palette that complements the garden's hues.

1) PRETTY IN PINK, this outdoor living room features a pastel palette to complement the soft cottage architecture and neutral gray and white palette of the outbuilding that serves as the room's backdrop. Vintage metal garden chairs painted pink exude a cottage charm with a youthful exuberance. It's no coincidence that even the garden's flowers are predominantly pink.

2) THE POTTING SHED carves out more than one living room outdoors, and each sustains the pastel pink palette. More vintage chairs painted pink soften the landscape and prepare the eye for the palette that unfolds inside the shed.

3) THE OPEN-SIDED potting shed takes its color cues from the flowers cut from the garden just outside: pink, with accents of white and green, making the space as soft as petals.

showing YOUR colors

1) PRIMARY COLORS make a bright splash in any outdoor room. Secluded from the house, this room with a red bench, blue pillow, and yellow vase doesn't conform to standard indoor colors. The room is striking its own strong tones that will hold their own even in this full-sun space.

2) COBALT BLUE and lemon yellow—the colors of sea and sky and a bright summer sun—offer a popular duo for outdoor rooms because of their presence in nature. Note the cobalt is a deeper interpretation of blue than many, to pop out even in the boldest sunlight.

③

④

⑤

3,4 & 5) COOL COLORS provide a psychological antidote to the outdoor heat, and this outdoor dining room ushers in the cool at every turn. Lavender, blue, and green, analogous colors (next-door neighbors) on the color wheel, suggest refreshing mountain streams, green woodlands, and misty mornings. Used in tandem, they also evoke a festive mood.

INDEX

resources

Here are just a few of the many sources for furniture and accessories to decorate your outdoor room.

Brown Jordan
1801 N. Andrews Ave.
Pompano Beach, FL 33069
954-960-1299
brownjordan.com
Manufacturer of outdoor furniture

Crate and Barrel
1860 W. Jefferson Ave.
Naperville, IL 60540
800-967-6696
crateandbarrel.com
Retailer of outdoor furnishings and garden accessories

Fire Designs
437 W. Wrightwood Ave.
Elmhurst, IL 60126
630-661-4788
firedesigns.net
Manufacturer of the Luminaria outdoor fireplace

Frontgate
5566 West Chester Rd.
West Chester, OH 45069
800-626-6488
frontgate.com
Retailer of outdoor furnishings and kitchen equipment

Glen Raven, Inc.
1831 N. Park Ave.
Glen Raven, NC 27217
336-227-6211
glenraven.com
Manufacturer of Sunbrella fabrics

Hearth Patio &
Barbecue Assoction
1601 N. Kent, Ste. 1001
Arlington, VA 22209
703-522-0086
hpba.org
Leading fireplace association with links to outdoor fireplace manufacturers

Outdoor Fabrics
P.O. Box 228172
Miami, FL 33122
800-640-3539
outdoorfabrics.com
Retailer of weather-resistant fabric sold by the yard

Restoration Hardware
15 Koch Rd., Ste. J
Corte Madera, CA 94925
800-762-1005
restorationhardware.com
Retailer of outdoor furniture and garden accessories

Shades of Light
and
Rugs Under Foot
4924 W. Broad St.
Richmond VA 23230
800-262-6612
shadesoflight.com
rugsunderfoot.com
Retailer of weather-resistant lamps and flooring

Smith and Hawken
P.O. Box 8690,
Pueblo, CO 81008
800-940-1170
smithandhawken.com
Retailer of outdoor furnishings and garden accessories

Vessel, Inc.
P.O. Box 470474
Brookline, MA 02447
877-805-1801
vesselinc.com
Manufacturer of the Candelas featured on page 202

Vieluxe
200 E. Daniels Rd.
Palatine, IL 60067
847-202-2724
vieluxe.com
Manufacturer of outdoor grills

Weatherend
6 Gordon Dr.
Rockland, ME 04841
800-456-6483
weatherend.com
Manufacturer of outdoor furniture

CREDITS:

Linens, pillows, and mirrors on pages 22-23 provided by:
Beekeeper's Cottage, 43738 Hay Rd., Ashburn, VA 20147. 703/726-9411

Landscaping on pages 22-23, 32-33, and 133 provided by:
Surreybrooke, 8537 Hollow Rd., Middletown, MD 21769. 301-371-7466
surreybrooke.com

Images of outdoor grills on pages 76-77 provided by Vieluxe

Image of portable outdoor fireplace on page 131 provided by Fire Designs

Images of outdoor lamps on page 203 provided by Shades of Light

Images of outdoor rugs and carpet samples on pages 165, 166 and 203 provided by Rugs Under Foot

Images of outdoor furniture on pages 188-189 courtesy of Brown Jordan

Image of outdoor lights on page 205 provided by Restoration Hardware

Images on pages 37, 114 bottom, and 123: Photographer, Jamie Hadley; Landscape Designer, Stephen Suzman; and Architect, Sandy Walker

Images on pages 72, 73: Photographer, Jay Graham, Landscape Designer, Robert Griffith; and Designer Wendy Calcaterra

Images on pages 93, 100, and 101 bottom: Photographer, Jay Graham, Landscape Architect, Laurence Fleury; and Plant Designer, Clair Bobrow